D1606543

Suicide's Aftermath: Three Griefs More!

Christian Couple's Compounded Grief for a Loved One's Suicide

by Charlie & Terry Liebert

This book is a work of non-fiction. Unless otherwise noted, the authors and publisher make no explicit guarantees as to the accuracy of the information contained in this book. The views expressed in this work are solely those of the authors.

Scripture quotations are from The Holy Bible, English Standard Version® (ESV®), copyright © 2001 by Crossway, a publishing ministry of Good News Publishers. Used by permission. All rights reserved. Some Scripture is also taken from the King James Version of the Bible, in public domain. Because of the dynamic nature of the Internet, any web addresses or links contained in this book may have changed since publication and may not be valid.

Acknowledgments

Thanks to Terry Perrone Liebert my wife and helpmate for 53 years for her patience in my frustrations and obstacles. She is a major contributor in direction and structure of this book. Her Biblical wisdom often exceeds mine and is of intense value to moving me forward in God's calls on my life. Her guidance in how to handle and structure of the Biblical sections was particularly helpful. BLESS you dear!

The cover photo was done by Courtney Nedimyer Photography in July 2018 for Charlie and Terry's 50th wedding anniversary celebration, August 3, 2018.

Terry and I thank God for His gracious salvation which we have lived together with for more than 45 years. Without the LORD and the Holy Spirit's imparted strength, I can say with certainty we could not have survived our loved one's death by suicide. I cannot imagine going through the *Three Grief's More!* without Jesus beside us.

Chapter 2. The Origin of Death. Reprinted with permission from "Without Three Miracles Darwin's Dead,"

Chapter 2. The Value of Human Life. Reprinted by permission from ANSWERS for: "The Hope that is in YOU."

Contributors

Two co-authors wrote narrative stories for this book: Cindie Brown, and Liz Woolley.

Cindie Brown wrote the story of her son, Stephen's life. When I asked her to write it, she became very excited because Stephens's story is one, she has long had a burden to tell. Cindie had to overcome major obstacles in writing it because she has been blind from her youth.

Stephen's life story tells of Jesus' GREAT redemption and His ability to save even the most lost sinners. Stephen became a believer at age 9 but at 18 drifted, like the prodigal son, off into a life of deep sin.

Multiple serious addictions and the "gay" life controlled his life patterns for more than 17 years. In his early 30s he came back to Christ, forsook the "gay" lifestyle but still struggled with one serious addiction. On the eve of going to a Christian year long program to help cure this addiction he died of an accidental overdose.

THANK YOU, Cindie for giving us this very powerful story of God's Amazing Grace. I commend Cindie and her husband Scot for their steadfast love for Stephen even when he was very far from God. They are a great example of how Christian parents should treat wayward children. Love them into the Kingdom! Judgement comes from God alone.

The other author who wrote a chapter (Shawn) is Liz Woolley founder of Online Gamers Anonymous (OLGA) after her son died by suicide because of addiction to a video game. I have published two books for the OLGA ministry. I am pleased to have her son's story included here. It shows addiction can wander into many areas even in Christian family's lives. Thanks, Liz, for giving us Shawn's story and your work with OLGA to bring hope to those addicted to video games and other forms of technology.

In Memoriam.

Dorothy Ellen Rose.	**11/11/1960**
Paul Chenoweth.	**02/15/1982**
Joseph Cedrone.	**06/25/1982**
Shawn Woolley	**11/20/2001**
Stephen Alan Brown.	**03/19/2017**

Table Of Contents

Preface, Why I Wrote this Book.

As a child, I went to church almost every Sunday. In Sunday School we learned many Bible stories, but I never remembered being confronted with the Gospel. At 16 years old, I became very aware of the hypocrisy of church members. One Sunday morning, the pastor was droning on about the evil of drinking any form of alcohol. Yet, I knew that most of the adults sitting around me had been at the Amityville Yacht Club raucous season-opening party, the night before consuming a lot of beer, wine, and liquor. I'd witnessed the party from my friend Mike's home across the creek from the club.

How foolish," I thought, "These people don't believe a word of what's being said! Hypocrites ALL!"

At that moment, I began to shut off anything the church had to say and accelerated my descent from being a marginal Christian to becoming a "hardcore" atheist.

By the time I was 24, approaching completion of my BS in Chemistry at Fairleigh Dickenson University, I had become an active evangelistic atheist. I asked, "How could there be a loving God with a world so filled with pain, suffering, and death?" No one I asked provided me with any reasonable answers I could accept. My Methodist Pastor told me these were "mysteries we just had to accept."

Forty years later in March 1977, I became a Christian at an Episcopal church sponsored retreat in Asheville, NC. My Christian testimony is in the Appendix. For the next 45 years God was preparing my wife Terry and me for the tragic events that came upon us on March 10, 2022, a close family members suicide.

There were several events involving death in my time as an atheist that pushed me further into that worldview. As the recent tragedy of suicide overtook Terry and I, we were spurred on to write this book to help Christian parents endure a loved one's sudden unexpected death by suicide. Suddenly confronted with this personal tragedy I faced two choices, 1) flee FROM God or 2) flee TO God. At the beginning of the Bible's book of Job, it shows you can react to tragic events by fleeing from or running to God. As the book begins, we find Job losing his children, his possessions, and his health in a very short time. The dialogue between Job and his wife in Job 2:8-10, illustrates his choices.

Flee FROM God. Job losing children, possessions, and personal health. "...sat down among the ashes. Then, his wife said, 'Do you still hold fast your integrity? Curse God and die.'" The choice here is clear: REJECT God's providential will and accept your own death as final, ending in the unknown.

Flee TO God. But he (Job) said to her, "You speak as one of the foolish women would speak. Shall we receive good from God, and **shall we not receive evil?**" In all this Job did not sin with his lips."

My choice was clear! Would I flee? What would I choose to do? Curse God? Abandon my faith? This choice was REAL! Forsake God OR in faith continue to follow Him. When Jesus' disciples were confronted with the question of whether to continue to follow Jesus they responded with, WHERE ELSE CAN WE GO??!!

John. 6:66-69 *After this (teaching) many of his disciples turned back and no longer walked with him. So, Jesus said to the twelve, "Do you want to go away as well?" Simon Peter answered him, "Lord, to whom shall we go? You have the words of eternal life, and we have believed, and have come to know, that you are the Holy One of God."*

Introduction. Three Levels of Grief.

The sudden unexpected death of an adult family member is always shocking, carrying us immediately into grief and mourning. This book will aid parents, particularly Christians, as they go through up to three additional steps of the mourning process that come from losing one's unbelieving family member to suicide. Understanding these additional three levels of grief will eventually lead them out of mourning to emerge back into the normal flow of life.

Ultimately, the source of death is SIN, as defined in the source of TRUTH, the Bible! No matter what the direct cause of anyone's death, sorrow immediately envelops the survivors. WE grieve because we know inside ourselves death is NOT the way the Universe was intended to be NOR how it was created NOR is it the way God wants it to work. We will talk more about this later as we discuss levels of grief.

There are three levels of grief that go beyond the death of a person that was expected and/or anticipated. Our grief intensifies at each level as we consider sudden, unexpected death by suicide and each person's eternal destiny based on their relationship with Jesus. These three increasing levels of grief are

1) Grieving for <u>sudden, unexpected death</u> recognizing the source of death from the Scriptures. Genesis 3. "The Fall" was the entrance of SIN and DEATH. The original Creation had, NO DEATH.

2) Grieving for the special case of <u>death by suicide</u> and its unique impact on the survivors. Asking the "WHY" question. Shame?

3) Grieving by Christians for the death of <u>one who did not make a profession of faith in Christ.</u> Where are they now? HEAVEN or HELL?

1) Death: NOT Expected.

The first level of grief is mourning for sudden, unexpected deaths in our families. Accidents are the number one cause of death for ages 10 to 40 and the number three cause for ages 45-54. Natural causes, like diseases or organ failure are only a small portion of <u>sudden or unexpected death</u>. The "IF only?" and the "What IF?" questions come up as we react to its surprise appearance.

The two more levels of grief are escalations because of specific circumstances. Second, is death by suicide. Third, is Christians grieving for the death of an unbeliever because it opens the question of their eternal destiny-HEAVEN or HELL?

2) Death: BY Suicide

Suicide is an act of the human will working from a mind in great desperation that sees no escape from the current life conditions. It is a sin, self-murder, from which you cannot repent. It causes an additional level of mourning in the survivors because it evokes a question that doesn't apply to previous levels; "**Why** did they do it?" "**Why** now?" "Didn't they realize it would hurt all that love them?" Grieving expands to include the persons mental, and emotional health, and behavior factors. In addition to our grief, we must deal even further with the "What IF" questions and our "IF Only" responses. Suicide makes the mourning process longer, more difficult, more complex and it raises, "WHY?" questions we don't want to answer. In the U.S. suicide contains a negative stigma that may even break family and friend relationships.

3) Death: WITHOUT Faith.

This third additional level of grief is confined to Christians who accept Jesus' statements that he is the ONLY way to the Father.

John 6:44 "No one can come to me unless the Father who sent me draws him. And I will raise him up on the last day"

John 6:65 And he said, "This is why I told you that no one can come to me unless it is granted him by the Father."

Those that die in Christ have secure futures. Initially their death brings survivors grief but ends in rejoicing because we KNOW they are with the LORD.

2 Corinthians 2:6-10. So, we are always of good courage. We know that while we are at home in the body we are away from the Lord, for we walk by faith, not by sight. Yes, we are of good courage, and we would rather be away from the body and at home with the Lord. So, whether we are at home or away, we make it our aim to please him. For we must all appear before the judgment seat of Christ, so that each one may receive what is due for what he has done in the body, whether good or evil.

Psalm 116:15 "Precious in the sight of the LORD is the death of his saints."

We believe that when unbelievers die, they go to the place of the dead (Seoul in Hebrew) and will be cast into the Lake of Fire, at the final judgment, called the Second Death.

Revelation 20:13b-15. Death and Hades gave up the dead who were in them, and they were judged, each one of them, according to what they had done. Then Death and Hades were thrown into the lake of fire. This is the second death, the lake of fire. And if anyone's name was not found written in the book of life, he was thrown into the lake of fire...."

Here is an analogy that helps understand these three additional steps in the grieving process. A sudden death is like a wound in the inside of your arm, slashed from elbow to wrist. It's shocking, painful, and requires immediate attention. At first it seems unreal because you are in shock but quickly you come to full understanding your arm is slashed (moving toward the realization your loved one is dead). Initially, it hurts a LOT!! When you come to fully realize you've been injured, the pain (grief) begins. (Now, you fully realize your loved one is dead.) Like a real wound it needs immediate attention, disinfection, stitches, and bandages. For your loved one's death, they need arrangements, a funeral, and a burial. Then, you enter a period of mourning and grief, and the wound healing begins. When you look at it, it still hurts. Remembrance brings on renewed grief. As the wound heals, the pain subsides and eventually scar forming begins. Time allows the grieving to eventually pass but the scar will always be there. In a sense, we get over the death, but we really don't fully forget because we see the scar and that scar remains with us for the rest of our life.

This book's content is strongly influenced by Charlie's life, first as an atheist (1941-1977) and then as a Christian (1978-Present). Outlined below are the significant events that influenced his worldview in each era.

My life as an atheist.

After graduating High School in 1959, I left my childhood beliefs as a marginal Christian and began evolving into a materialistic atheist. I attended church with my parents and sisters until I was 16. We went to church every Sunday but as I became a teenager my skepticism of Christianity grew. I had many questions about the faith, but I could find no one with answers. By the time I was 20, in 1961, all childhood faith was gone, and I was a "hardcore" atheist. Here are the major events that shaped my strong atheist worldview. MY conclusions from these events are in caps.

• 1957 -The hypocrisy of church adults sitting around me on Sunday morning nodding to the preacher's prohibition sermon while many were suffering the effects of ragging hangovers from Amityville Yacht Club's raucous party the night before. HYPOCRITES ALL!

• 1959 - The broken relationship with my first girlfriend was abrupt and painful. GOD DOESN'T CARE!

• 1960 - Paul, one of my best friend's, girlfriend Dorothy, 18, died suddenly of a cerebral hemorrhage. I was the only one from our high school clique who was still in Amityville in 1960. I mourned with Paul for three days. As a result of Dorothy's death, Paul became an alcoholic and would take his own life in 1982. Dorothy's death was one of the major events that pushed me to profess atheism. DEATH EVEN TAKES THE YOUNG AND INNOCENT.

• 1963 - I lost a bunch of "buddies" in the Fire Department when I responded emotionally to a frivolous event. My own fault but very painful. THE WORLD IS FULL OF BROKEN RELATIONSHIPS AND PEOPLE BEHAVING BADLY.

• 1976 - The suicide of a 16-year-old neighbor's child in Greensboro, NC. DEATH FOR ALL IS REAL AND KNOWS NO AGE LIMIT!

14

My life as a Christian.

After becoming a believer in 1977, Jesus brought many dramatic changes to my life that are described in my testimony in the Appendix. After becoming a Christian six sudden unexpected deaths affected my life: Paul, Joe, Kenny, Stephen, Shawn and my loved one.

- 1982 – Paul, one of my high school buddies dies by suicide. He lost his girlfriend, Dorothy in 1960. Her death and my mourning with Paul is a major turning point toward atheism

- 1982 - Joe - One of my co-workers, who I was very close to, died by suicide. We both started working at JR Geigy Co., on the same day and worked together for 15 years. Joe was a treasured friend.

- 2009 – Rennie - My father-in-law, Rennie's, death was on 12/25 at 10:25 am. He had lived with us for more than 11 years. This is the only person I've seen die.

- 2015 - Kenny Ray Handy, my children's friend from Wesleyan Christian Academy in High Point, NC, took his life because of a failing business. Kenny had all the hallmarks of a true Christian believer.

- 2016 - Shawn - Writing Shawn Woolley's biography for the ministry On-line Gamers Anonymous (OLGA) with John Michael Langel, Jr., and Liz Woolley I learned, the suicide connection, the desperation, and the emptiness of video game addiction.

- 2017 - Stephen – Stephen Brown was my workshop and seminar helper for three years. After taking on the "gay" lifestyle and many serious addictions, he accidently overdosed on cocaine. Stephen's death, although accidental was sudden and unexpected.

- 2022 – A close family member died by suicide in March 2022.

Chapter 1. Charlie's Descent to Atheism.

Boy Scout Summer Camp 1952

Top row, center Scoutmaster Emile Anderson, fifth from right, Stewart. Middle row from right, Eddie, unknown, Charlie, Carleton

Amityville Memorial High School, 1959

There was a group of eight guys that hung out together in my High School years on Long Island at Amityville Memorial High School: Charlie (me) Paul, Carleton, Russell, John, Stewart, Mike, and Ed. Occasionally John's brother Pete joined us.

Charlie.   Paul.   Carleton.

Russell.   John.   Stewart.

NO PICTURE

Ed   John's Brother Pete   Mike.

I became skeptical about the Christian faith at 16 and by the time I was 18, I expected my religious view would become atheistic. The death of Dorothy Ellen Rose is the singular event that most solidified my atheistic beliefs. After she died, I asked, "How could a good and loving God allow such pain and suffering?" By the time I was 20, I was certain God couldn't exist. Come back with me now to 1959 to see my turning point event. I'll turn 18 on September 2, 1960.

This group of guys crossed over a lot in dating different girls from our school and girls from a nearby high school in Seaford. One girl might go out with Carleton one week and Russ the next. For us guys, Friday night was guys poker night and Saturday was date night. Most of the girls we dated had curfews at midnight, so as a group, with our dates on Saturday, we'd go to a movie, outdoor theater, ice cream shop, pizza parlor, minigolf, house parties, Gilgo Beach bonfires, and occasionally a Long Island concert.

We'd drop the girls off at their homes and then approaching midnight the guys would meet at the Amityville Diner for coffee and pie or later at the Village Tavern for beer and pretzels. We graduated from diner to tavern when the two oldest of us turned 18, Russ and Carleton. The "drinking age" was 18. The bartenders knew not all of us were 18 so they would check the age proof of the two who were, Carleton and Russ. Then say, "OK that's enough." And let the rest of us in that were underage. Local authorities did not enforce this law, so, their only fear was a state inspector, but they scheduled their visits. If there was an inspection scheduled a little sign would be in the outside door's window that said NO NUTS TODAY. That sign appeared once every three months, but we checked every time before we went in to be sure no inspector was there. Tap draft beers were 15 cents, bottles a quarter and most of the time the pretzels were free in bowls on the bar. Some weekends they'd have peanuts in the shell in bowls for 25 cents a bowl with one bowl refill. Peanut shells went on the floor, so the floor got "crunchy."

Dorothy.

When it came to dating, there was one couple in our group that was different. Paul and Dorothy started dating when Paul was a high school sophomore. They fell in love and were devoted to each other through his two remaining high school years. Neither of them ever dated anyone else. One night we were leaving a pirate movie when Stewart, our Jewish member, said, "Paul and Dorothy are the only couple that is truly a couple. The rest of us are just loose cannons in a storm-tossed ship bouncing from girl to girl." We all tacitly agreed he was right by giving nods and responding with "Yeah." That was life in 1958.

John Toomey Photo
1960 Mack B 750
Amityville N.Y., Chem. Hose 3, 1-1-3

When I turned 16, I joined the Amityville Fire Department's Chemical Hose Company #3 as a junior fire fighter. Juniors were given a helmet, raincoat, and boots so we'd be recognized at a fire scene as a fire fighter. We were not allowed to go more than 50 feet from our assigned vehicle at any fire scene unless ordered to by a regular officer. The officers often had us getting coffee and sometimes snacks. We were allowed to ride on the truck to fire scenes but couldn't drive it until we were 18 and we took the driver training.

We became FULL volunteer firemen on our 18th birthday in an exotic ceremony. We often had fireman's parties with beer at the fire house. Since my dad was German, I drank beer since I was about 12 so it was not a big deal to have a couple of beers at firehouse parties even when I was 16 or 17.

During my junior year in high school, I stopped going to church and joined the Saturday and Sunday Firemen's Pinochle Club. Between 8 or 12, in tables of four, would play Pinochle, on Saturday afternoon after having a spectacular roast beef deli sandwich for lunch. On Sunday we played starting at 11:00 but usually only one table of four fireman and no deli sandwich since it was closed on Sunday. The "blue" laws were still in effect in those days.

The graduating class from Amityville Memorial High School of June 1959 included Carleton, John, Russ, Stewart, Paul, and me. The graduating class of June 1960 included Mike and Ed. Paul's girlfriend Dorothy Rose was scheduled to graduate in the class of 1961. By the fall of 1960, Paul, Dorothy, and myself were still living in Amityville. Everyone else in our clique went to college "out of town." I went to SUNY (State University of New York) at Farmingdale, which was a short commute, so I still lived at my parent's home.

Paul's dad was a builder of custom sailboats and Paul was being apprenticed by his dad to take over the business. Dorothy, when not in school, was with them as Paul was being trained. She wanted to help build the boats after they were married. They were working toward a wedding date in the summer of 1961, after school finished.

On Saturday, November 12, 1960, I got my usual lunch roast beef sandwich at the deli and walked into the firehouse entrance to turn left into the truck area. At the end of that entry hall was the police desk and sitting there was a good friend Sargent Eddie Baxter.

Eddie looked up when he heard me and said, "Hey, Charlie come here."

"Yeah, OK" I said as I walked up to the desk. "What's up?"

"Do you know what happened last night?"

I said, "Did I miss a fire call?"

I could see pain on Eddies' face as he slowly said, "No, Dorothy Rose died last night of what the coroner thinks was a cerebral hemorrhage."

I exclaimed, "WHAT?" I'd heard what he said but my comprehension was not complete.

Eddie saw I didn't fully understand so he repeated, "Dorothy Rose, your friend, Paul's girlfriend died last night of a cerebral hemorrhage."

I stood dazed for several seconds to let comprehension sink in. Then I thought, Paul! I turned closer to Eddie and almost shouted, "Did Paul get there before she died?"

Tears welled up in his eyes as he said. "He arrived about ten minutes too late. It was a terrible scene. I'll remember it the rest of my life. She was only 16. Paul took it very hard. He knelt by the bed weeping for over an hour. We had to forcibly remove him when the coroner arrived. Even then he wouldn't be comforted."

I knew I was the only one of our school group of guys left in town that could help carry Paul through this crisis. I immediately took responsibility by going to Paul's home. I knocked on the front door. His mom answered, recognized me, and said, "He's in the back yard." She immediately closed the door. I stood there for a second puzzled and then went to the driveway to go to the backyard. I saw Paul sitting on a chair on the edge of the dock. (Their backyard ended at the dock of the canal that led to the Great South Bay.) As I approached, I could see his shoulders shaking from his sobbing.

I called, "Paul, it's Charlie."

Paul leaped out of the chair and ran to hug me but continued crying. As we stood there together, I saw his mother look out the window and quickly turn away. He said, "We can talk now."

I said, "Sure." His crying somewhat subsided.

I pulled up a chair on the edge of the dock and said "I came as soon as I found out about Dorothy. I was going to play Pinochle at the fire house when Eddie Baxter told me what happened..." Paul interrupted.

"Oh, yeah. He was there last night." He started to cry again, and I cried with him. We sat silently for several minutes with just the sound of the creek water washing against the dock. I didn't know what to do next.

I said, "All the other guys in our group are away at school so I'll stay with you for the next couple of days." I had no idea how difficult these next three days would be.

Dorothy's funeral arrangements were for visitation on Thursday and Friday from 1:00-5:00 PM and 7:00-9:30 PM. Saturday's visitation was from 11:00 AM - 1:00 PM, then, the procession to the cemetery began. A graveside service with internment began at 2:00 PM.

On Thursday I arrived at the funeral home at 12:45 to meet Paul. He was already there when I arrived, and we went in together immediately. Paul went over knelt at the coffin and started to cry. I went over and put my hand on his shoulder.

He placed his hand on her forehead, looked up at me and said, "Charlie she's dead. Her body's here but she's gone." He laid his hand on her forehead. "She's cold!" We both sat in folding chairs just above the head of the coffin.

This was the first time I saw a person "laid out" and it was shocking to me. She looked the same as she had the last time, we had pizza. yet she was dead and cold.

I'd been drifting away from Christianity and the church since I was sixteen, but at this moment, looking at the dead Dorothy, I made a certain, sure decision that there can't be a good, loving God who would allow this to happen. My descent to atheism was well underway. I would repeat my mantra for many years, "There is NO GOD!" So, Charlie the ATHEIST began to emerge.

About 2:30, Paul was talking to several of Dorothy's girlfriends, so I went outside the building for a smoke. I walked out into a beautiful fall day with bright sunshine and the smell of salt air from the bay. I stopped in shock! I asked no one in particular: "How can it be so beautiful here and just 10 feet away is pain, suffering and death?"

As I expected no one answered.

Paul's mother came out and came directly to me, "Charlie, Paul's dad and I are concerned that he may be suicidal so can you stay with him when he's not with one of us or when we are not at home?"

"Sure." I said, without thinking what that commitment might entail. We closed that night at 9:30 PM.

As agreed, the next day I met Paul at the funeral home at 12:30. We sat again by the coffin. I went out for a smoke about 2:00 PM again. When I returned, his seat was occupied by one of Dorothy's friends. I asked, "Where's Paul?"

She looked up at me, "He said he needed to be alone, so he said he was going to Gilgo."

My body stiffened. I'd promised his mom I'd stay with Paul and now he'd gone to Gilgo Beach which was on the barrier island that separates the Great South Bay from the Atlantic Ocean, about half hours' drive away. Our whole group and about 20 others, 40 in all, had been at Gilgo last summer for a bonfire on the beach to celebrate our graduation. We'd been caught in a summer thunderstorm and saw lightning strike the dunes near us. This is when Carleton got his petrified lightning or fulgurite.

I asked myself, "Was Paul going back there to drown himself? Or, just to reminisce past events?" I panicked.

"I have to go find him!" I blurted out to the girls.

I arrived in the Gilgo parking lot less than 30 minutes later. I saw Paul's car parked in the eastern corner of the lot. He drove a 1950 Pontiac that he'd painted bright blue, so I knew he was here. I thought, "Where would he go?"

I remembered the bonfire. The pit was about ¼ mile east down the beach. I took off my shoes, and socks, and headed down the beach. As I crested a dune, I saw Paul sitting on a one of the pieces of driftwood that encircled the fire pit. He saw me coming, waved, but just sat there looking at the ocean. As I approached, he looked up and said, "My mom sent you, didn't she?"

"Not really, but she asked me to stay with you for the next few days. You should have told me where you were going." I replied.

"I wanted to be alone to try to understand what happened. I don't know what I'll do without Dorothy." He started to cry.

I joined him crying. We sat in silence for a long time. As I looked around some of the memories of that place came back. I finally asked, "Do you remember the last time we were here?"

"Yes, I do." He smiled for the first time since I saw him on the dock at his home the day after she died. I looked at my watch. It was almost 3:00 PM.

We both relived the last three years of our lives together on that cold windy beach. We laughed, cried, rejoiced, and sighed for the next 2½ hours. He talked about Dorothy being the only one for him and he made fun of the three different girlfriends I had dated in High School.

I said, "But now I am working on number four."

Finally, I said, "It's almost 5:30. We need to go now if we are going to be at the funeral home at 7:00."

We walked back to the cars. He said, "Let's stop at the Massapequa Diner and get a burger on the way back."

While eating at the diner, Paul with tears in his eyes said, "Charlie, thanks for coming. I feel much better after our time at the beach. I'll always remember your care."

At the viewing that evening and the next day Paul was much more at ease greeting well-wishers and mourners. I remember little about the graveside service or burial except throwing a handful of dirt into the grave. In my mind was one thought. "God does NOT exist! How could He with all this suffering and pain? We are all alone and death is our only destiny!"

Paul.

In 1961, I took a job in New Jersey after graduating SUNY Farmingdale but moved back to my parent's home in April 1963. The company my dad worked for went out of business. My parents needed money to pay the mortgage, or they would lose the family home. I couldn't let that happen. Until late 1965, I would pay monthly rent, to my parents, to keep the bank at bay.

31 Richmond Ave, Amityville, NY. Family Home 1944-2001
I commuted daily to Edgewater N.J. from Amityville, N.Y. Stepping on the LIRR (Long Island Railroad) train at the Amityville station at 5:45 AM and stepping off the Fire Island Express Bar Car back in Amityville at 7:02 PM.

1959 Amityville LIRR Station. Village Tavern background right

Since the Village Tavern was a short walk from the train station, dinner was often beer and pretzels.

I didn't see Paul again for three years, until 1963. On a Saturday morning in September 1963, our home phone rang at 2:30 AM. I woke and was about to go back to sleep when my dad came into my room turned on the light and said, "That was Bill Kay on the phone. He needs our help. Let me tell you what he said."

Bill Kay was a very good friend of my dad who had been "best man" at my parents' wedding. Now, he was chief of police for the Amityville Village Police Department. My dad related the conversation.

Bill: "Hello. Joe, its Bill Kay.

Joe (Dad): "Hello, what's up at 2:30 AM?

Bill: "Joe, I need your help. We have had a very busy night with a major wreck on Sunrise Highway. A rash of drunk drivers has our four-cell jail full. I've got all my resources tied up clearing the accident. So, I can't deal with Paul, a good friend of Charlie, who was picked up drunk on the street outside Village Tavern. Can you come here to get him and then get him home?

Joe: "I'll bring Charlie and we'll be there in about 10 minutes"

Bill, startled: "What's Charlie doing here?"

Joe: "He's been living here for the last six months."

Bill: "OK bring him along. We are trying to sober him up with coffee but he's still very intoxicated."

We picked up Paul and walked him in our driveway for two hours to get him sober enough to take him home. That was the last time I saw him.

In March 1982, nineteen years later, Carleton's wife Gail called to tell me Paul committed suicide a month before, in February 1982. She said he never recovered from Dorothy's death and suffered from various forms of addiction and depression all those years. By this time, I had been a Christian for more than 5 years. I had a long cry for Paul's life of desperation and hopelessness. I then a hearty laugh at my foolish time as an atheist. *The fool has said in his heart there is No God! Palm 14:1*

Amityville Memorial 1959 50th Reunion

Already deceased, Paul and Mike.

Charlie, Eddie, Stewart, John

Gail and Carleton.   **Kathy and Russ.**

Shelly.

My family moved from Rockland County, NY to Greensboro, NC in 1973. We lived in a neighborhood that had homes built back-to-back, so we shared yards with our back neighbors. We joined a neighborhood Bridge Club and came to know some of them and their children. One of the neighborhood men was a very busy surgeon that loved breakfast at I Hop (International House of Pancakes). Four of us went there with him about once a month. One Saturday, he expressed concern for his 17-year-old daughter, Shelly. She had always been an unhappy child. She'd had relationships with several boys that had ended badly. She often complained about being bullied by other girls at school. In the last two years, Shelly had made multiple suicide attempts. Several weeks after he shared his concern, she took her own life. I went to the viewing and funeral, but the burial.

When I saw her in the coffin, I was immediately taken back to Dorothy. The remembrance of those "Dorothy" days was in my mind often to confirm my atheism. I relived the moment I threw that handful of earth into Dorothy's grave. Later, I would wonder if my atheism was shaken at that time. I remember asking in my mind, "Is this really all there is?" At that time, I had no answer, YET!

Chapter 2. Worldview: Death and Life.

We will define now, for the reader, two different views of the origin of death and the value of human life for the atheist and the Christian.

The Origin of Death.

Evolution advances by the natural processes of 1) mutation and 2) Natural Selection These processes operate for millions of generations of living organisms that reproduce, struggle, and die.

Evolution's view of DEATH:
- **An essential part of Evolution's creative force.**
- **Has always been here & will be until the end of time.**

One conclusion that is often drawn from Atheistic Evolution is that although we have a physical body that is alive, its only interactions are chemical and electrical. YOU HAVE NO SELF! Your life is an illusion. You and everything around you are not real! This is in direct contradiction to what the Bible teaches. It says we have life in our soul that includes three parts: a mind (intelligence), emotions (feelings), and will (making decisions to act). That complete soul life sets us apart from all other kinds of living organisms.

God the Creator gave us a three-fold nature: the physical body, life or soul, and spirit. The spirit part of man died when Adam sinned. We get that spiritual life partially back when we become believers and receive the Holy Spirit. Our spirit will not be fully restored until we get our resurrection bodies, and our sinful nature is purged away. That's why Paul could say in *Romans 7:24-25 "Wretched man that I am! Who will deliver me from this body of death? Thanks be to God through Jesus Christ our Lord! So then, I myself serve the law of God with my mind, but with my flesh, I serve the law of sin."*

Let me illustrate. I am watching a nature program on the Discovery Channel. The lion stalks the herd of zebras and eventually takes down an older zebra, kills it and starts to eat it. What is the reaction of the other zebras in the herd, they are indifferent! They do not grieve for another creature's death. They continue their life as if nothing extraordinary happened. As a human, when someone we love dies, we grieve. Why? If we are just chemistry and electricity, then grieving is the height of foolishness. Our friend or relative just lost the battle of biology to the forces of chemistry. Life is gone and the body begins to decompose, yet because we are made in God's image, we KNOW that death is not right. God built into every man and woman a conscience that tells us what's right or wrong and it also tells us death is not what should happen. It is NOT what God intended for mankind. According to Scripture, death is an intruder. Death came to us all because of Adam's original sin and our own sin in both nature and action. We know, as Christians by faith, that death will be destroyed at the last judgment. God will banish it from Creation. That's NOT biology or chemistry. That's who we are as humans' beings made in God's image. We are unique and superior to all the other animals. For animals, when death comes, they return to the Earth and go out of existence. Men are everlasting. When we die, we enter eternity with God in Heaven, or we leave his presence and perish in Hell. Read Romans Chapters 1-3.

Biblical / Creation view of DEATH:
- **an intruder, caused by SIN**
- **not part of the biblical created order**
- **began at "The Fall." Genesis 3**
- **will have its end in the lake of fire. Revelation 20**
- **NOT in humankind's creation. Genesis 1-2.**
- **NOT in humankind's destiny. Revelation 21-22.**

The basic difference between the views is that in atheism DEATH is part of the Universe and is PERMANENT! It always has been and always will be. The Christian view is that DEATH is an intrusion, is TEMPORARY and has both a BEGINNING and an END.

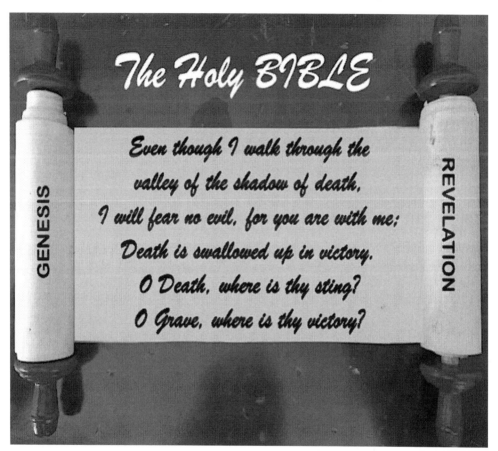

The Holy BIBLE

GENESIS

REVELATION

Even though I walk through the
valley of the shadow of death,
I will fear no evil, for you are with me;
Death is swallowed up in victory.
O Death, where is thy sting?
O Grave, where is thy victory?

DEATH's Purpose

The atheist/evolution model has death as an integral part of the process while in the Christian/Creation model it is a temporary intruder that has a beginning and an end. Therefore, we ask the question, "What is deaths purpose in each model? By examining Death's purpose, we will see even more clearly the contrast between belief and unbelief.

In Atheistic Evolution:

Here's a Q&A from the Smithsonian Institution.

"How are humans and monkeys related?

Humans and monkeys are both primates. But humans are *not* descended from monkeys or any other primate living today. We do share a common ape ancestor with chimpanzees. It lived between 8 and 6 million years ago. But humans and chimpanzees evolved differently from that same ancestor. All apes and monkeys share a more distant relative, which lived about 25 million years ago."

How many generations of developing chimp/man will it take in the seven million years Evolution requires for chimps and men to evolve from the common ancestor. We'll use a generation of 15 years from parent birth to first childbirth as reasonable. We start with two pairs, so we have genetic diversity among the next generation. Then with each generation we take the progeny produced and add two new ones to continue the diversity. WE conclude that each generation must contain a minimum of eight individuals to make Evolution move forward toward chimps or men. We need at least 16 for the two paths to chimps and men. How many generations of 15 years in seven million years? 7,000,000 / 15 = 466,666! That means the absolute minimum of transition creatures is 466,666 times 16 = 7.5 million! So, 7.5 million transitions had to live, reproduce, and die for chimps and men evolve separately from a common ancestor. This analysis clearly shows the essential requirement of death so each generation to move forward. If there was no death the process would have to stop after 3 or 4 generations as survival resources would be depleted by the surviving first and second generations."

Evolution is a continuous process beginning with birth, survival, reproduction and then death. Death is one of the four forces required for the process to move forward.

DEATH must be present from the time life appears. DEATH is a creative force to move evolution forward.

In Biblical Creation:
The Original Creation was perfect with NO death.
Genesis 1:31. And God saw everything he had made and behold, it was very good (perfection is implied in the original Hebrew.)

God put Adam and Eve in the Garden of Eden and planted all the trees they would need to live forever. However, there was one tree they were not to eat from.

Genesis 1:9 And out of the ground the LORD God made to spring up every tree that is pleasant to the sight and good for food. The tree of life was in the midst of the garden, and the tree of the knowledge of good and evil.

The tree of life was there so they would not age or weaken. The tree of the knowledge of good and evil is a test of; 1) their obedience to God's rule and 2) their love for God himself which implies a threat of justice to be executed with disobedience.

Genesis 2-15-17. Then the LORD God took the man and placed him in the Garden of Eden to cultivate and keep it. And the LORD God commanded him, "You may eat freely from every tree of the garden, but you must not eat from the tree of the knowledge of good and evil; for in the day that you eat of it, you will surely die."

The PUNITIVE PENALTY for eating from that tree, to satisfy God's JUSTICE is DEATH. Adam failed the test of the tree and received the just penalty, death. This action, commonly called, "The Fall" is the point at which death enters the Creation in Genesis chapter 3, as an intruder, NOT intended and NOT part of the original design.

1 Corinthians 15:21-26 For as by a man came death, by a man has also come the resurrection of the dead. For as in Adam all die, so also in Christ shall all be made alive. But each in his own order: Christ the first fruits, then at his coming those who belong to Christ. Then comes the end, when he delivers the kingdom to God the Father after destroying every rule and every authority and power. For he must reign until he has put all his enemies under his feet. The last enemy to be destroyed is death. (Revelation chapter 20)

All humans are judged against God's standard.
Revelation 20:11-15. Then I saw a great white throne and him who was seated on it. From his presence earth and sky fled away, and no place was found for them. And I saw the dead, great and small, standing before the throne, and books were opened. Then another book was opened, which is the book of life. And the dead were judged by what was written in the books, according to what they had done. And the sea gave up the dead who were in it, Death and Hades gave up the dead who were in them, and they were judged, each one of them, according to what they had done. Then, Death and Hades were thrown into the lake of fire. This is the second death, the lake

of fire. And if anyone's name was not found written in the book of life, he was thrown into the lake of fire

DEATH is destroyed in the Lake of Fire.

Revelation 21:1-4 Then I saw a new heaven and a new earth, for the first heaven and the first earth had passed away, and the sea was no more. And I saw the holy city, new Jerusalem, coming down out of heaven from God, prepared as a bride adorned for her husband. And I heard a loud voice from the throne saying, "Behold, the dwelling place of God is with man. He will dwell with them, and they will be his people, and God himself will be with them as their God. He will wipe away every tear from their eyes, and death shall be no more, neither shall there be mourning, nor crying, nor pain anymore, for the former things have passed away."

Romans 8:22. We know that the whole creation has been groaning together in the pains of childbirth until the present time.

DEATH reigns from Genesis 3 until Revelation 20.

*Revelation 20:11-15 Then, I saw a great white throne and the One God, prepared as a bride adorned for her husband. And I heard a loud voice from the throne saying, "Behold, the dwelling place of God is with man. He will dwell with them, and they will be his people, and God himself will be with them as their God. He will wipe away every tear from their eyes, **and death shall be no more**, neither shall there be mourning, nor crying, nor pain anymore, for the former things have passed away."*

The Value of Human Life.

Reprinted from ANSWERS for: "The Hope that is in YOU."

Evolution and creation portray the value of human life in very different ways. In evolution, humanity is the highest animal, having no, special position above other animals. In some cases, animals are even regarded as equal to or even better than humans. People for the Ethical Treatment of Animals (PETA), an animal rights organization, rejects speciesism (the concept that one species is superior to any other) and the idea of animals as property. PETA opposes the use of animals in any form: as food, clothing, entertainment, or research subjects. The most famous statement of Ingrid E. Newkirk, co-founder, and president of PETA is, "When it comes to feelings like hunger, pain, and thirst, a rat is a pig is a dog is a boy." Note in that statement the equivalency of men to animals.

In contrast, in Creation, humanity is made in God's image, uniquely and special, because humans are designed to love and worship God. God gave humankind dominion over everything created. When Adam and Eve rebelled in the fall, they lost the spiritual communion they had with God and their spirits died. God made them for purpose, but because of their rebellion, God's condemnation fell on them both because of His perfect justice which brings eternal separation from him in Hell. God Himself, however, provides a way to escape this punishment by coming to earth himself as Jesus. Jesus pays the debt brought by that condemnation as our substitute and offers reconciliation to God to those who believe. In his resurrection, He affirms the new life available to all who believe. In Creation, then, human life is precious and unique but separated from God by sin. Christians return to that spiritual communion with God through the new birth and the gift of the Holy Spirit, yet they remain sinners saved by grace. At the believer's resurrection, they will receive a new, incorruptible body.

"I tell you this, brothers: flesh and blood cannot inherit the kingdom of God, nor does the perishable inherit the imperishable. Behold! I tell you a mystery. We shall not all sleep, but we shall all be changed, in a moment, in the twinkling of an eye, at the last trumpet. For the trumpet will sound, and the dead will be raised imperishable, and we shall be changed. For this perishable body must put on the imperishable, and this mortal body must put on immortality. When the perishable puts on the imperishable, and the mortal puts on immortality, then shall come to pass the saying that is written:

"Death is swallowed up in victory." "O death, where is your victory? O death, where is your sting?" The sting of death is sin, and the power of sin is the law. But thanks be to God, who gives us the victory through our Lord Jesus Christ.

Therefore, my beloved brothers, be steadfast, immovable, always abounding in the work of the Lord, knowing that in the Lord your labor is not in vain." (1 Corinthians 15:50–58)

Creation's Value of Human Life.

The Bible values human life the highest of all living organisms. Men and women are created in God's image with a three-fold nature: body, soul, and spirit. I'll use the Westminster Shorter Catechism to define man's position in relation to God. I've chosen it because I'm most familiar with it. I am not trying to get into denominational issues by using it so, for my Baptist brethren, I could just as easily have used the London Confession of 1789. Note: I've selected here only the questions from the Catechism that relate directly to the value of human life. The four parts of humanity's precious Biblical value are:

1) Creation in a perfect state for a purpose.

2) Established in a covenant relationship with God predicated on Adam and Eve's obedience.

3) Adam's disobedience resulting in alienation and separation from God bringing the entrance of sin and

4) Restoration to God by Christ because God loves his created men and women.

1) Creation in a perfect state for a purpose.

Q1: What is the chief end of man?

A1: Man's chief end is to glorify God, and to enjoy Him forever.

Q2: What rule hath God given to direct us how we may glorify and enjoy Him?

A2: The Word of God, contained in the Scriptures of the Old and New Testaments, is the only rule to direct us how we may glorify and enjoy Him.

Q3: What do the Scriptures principally teach?

A3: The Scriptures principally teach what man is to believe concerning God, and what duty God requires of man.

Q10: How did God create man?

A10: God created man male and female, after his image, in knowledge, righteousness, and holiness, with dominion over the creatures.

2) Established in a covenant relationship with God predicated on obedience.

Q12: What special act of providence did God exercise toward man in the estate wherein he was created?

A12: When God had created man, he entered a covenant of life with him, upon condition of perfect obedience; forbidding him to eat of the tree of the knowledge of good and evil, upon the pain of death.

3) Adam's disobedience resulting in alienation and separation from God.

Q13: Did our first parents continue in the estate wherein they were created?

A13: Our first parents, being left to the freedom of their own will, fell from the estate wherein they were created, by sinning against God.

Q16: Did all mankind fall in Adam's first transgression?

A16: The covenant being made with Adam, not only for himself, but for his posterity; all mankind, descending from him by ordinary generation, sinned in him, and fell with him, in his first transgression.

Q17: Into what estate did the fall bring mankind?

A17: The fall brought mankind into an estate of sin and misery.

Q18: Wherein consists of the sinfulness of that estate whereinto man fell.

A18: The sinfulness of that estate whereinto man fell, consists in the guilt of Adam's first sin, the want of original righteousness, and the corruption of his whole nature, which is commonly called Original Sin; together with all actual transgressions which proceed from it.

Q19: What is the misery of that estate whereinto man fell?

A19: All mankind, by their fall, lost communion with God is under his wrath and curse and so made liable to all miseries in this life to death itself and to the pains of hell forever.

4) Restoration to God by Christ because God loves His created men and women.

Q20. Did God leave all mankind to perish in the estate of sin and misery?

A20. God, having out of His mere good pleasure from all eternity, elected some to everlasting life. He entered a covenant of grace, to deliver them out of the estate of sin and misery, and to bring them into an estate of salvation by a Redeemer.

Q21: Who is the Redeemer of God's elect?

A21: The only Redeemer of God's elect is the Lord Jesus Christ, who being the eternal Son of God, became man, and so was, and continues to be, God and man in two distinct natures and one person forever.

So, we conclude humanity was created perfect but lost that perfection in sin when Adam and Eve rebelled. God offers to restore that relationship through Jesus Christ. Every person is 1) a sinner by birth, as a son or daughter of Adam, and 2) by nature, because we sin every day!

"If we say that we have no sin, we deceive ourselves, and the truth is not in us. If we confess our sins, he is faithful and just to forgive us our sins, and to cleanse us from all unrighteousness. If we say that we have not sinned, we make him a liar, and his word is not in us." 1 John 1:8–10

Every person ever born will spend eternity in either Heaven or Hell. There is no other possibility! The debt of sin, death, must be paid either by the individual or by Jesus' death on the cross. Christians call this "substitutionary atonement." Christ's death in place of our own death!

6th Commandment: "You Shall Not Murder."

The next significant factor to consider in valuing human life is God's prescribed punishment for taking another's life. When God gave Moses the Ten Commandments, "You shall not murder" was the first "shall not." The first five were positive rules and the second five, negative. Murder here implies intent to kill, not an accidental death. Accidental death is dealt with in Scripture with sever punishments but murder itself is a capital crime; to take another's life intentionally is to forfeit your own! The capital punishment for murder shows how seriously God regards each person's life. Even the unborn are protected in Scripture.

"When men strive together and hit a pregnant woman so that her children come out, but there is no harm, the one who hit her shall surely be fined, as the woman's husband shall impose on him, and he shall pay as the judges determine. But if there is harm, then you shall pay life for life, eye for an eye, a tooth for a tooth, hand for hand, foot for foot, burn for burn, wound for wound, stripe for stripe." (Exodus 21:22–25)

It is a capital crime if a person causes a miscarriage. If the baby dies, that person is to be executed, "life for life." As a Christian, if you believe what the Bible just said, then abortion is a heinous crime! *Yes*, God regards all human life as precious, even the unborn. Human life has great value because humanity is created in God's image.

For God so loved the world, that He gave His only (begotten) Son, that whoever believes in Him should not perish, but have eternal life. (John 3:16)

Now we'll compare the biblical value of human life to Evolution's value.

Evolution's Value of Human Life.

Evolution begins with inanimate matter and brings us all the variety of life on earth through a branching tree. Life starts with biogenesis as dead chemicals come together to form the first one-celled organism from "pond scum." Then, for millions of years, creatures evolve by mutation and natural selection to higher and higher forms. Finally, an apelike ancestor gives birth to the first man and woman. Humanity, then, is just the last step in billions and billions of changes from the one-celled pond scum that develops into complete human beings. As Dr. Gish said: "From goo to you by way of the zoo." Although we are the best nature can do, we are just the highest animal, really nothing better than other animals below us. This creation of life by evolution is a continuous process of reproduction, struggle, and death. Death is an important part of the process that helps evolution move forward. If evolution is true, *then*:

➢ There is no need for God.

➢ There is no sin and no need for a Savior

➢ Today's medical science can't explain the source of guilt because humans are *guilty.*

➢ Moral values have *no* basis and life has *no* meaning.

➢ Man is not responsible for his actions because he's just a bunch of chemical and electrical processes.

➢ The Bible is not reliable, and Christianity must be false.

➢ Humans are the highest animal, and we have the same regard for human life as any other animal.

➢ Therefore, men can be selectively bred, aborted, murdered, etc., because of natural selection.

44

The Nazis believed they were helping evolution move forward by killing those who natural selection would eventually eliminate.

Before I get to what the evolutionists say themselves, I want to highlight how teaching this aspect of evolution impacts our children. In the United States public schools, evolution is taught as fact, and there is no room for any other explanation of how we got here. In 1995 I summarized in a booklet I published, what we are teaching students in public schools about where they came from.

"You came from pond scum. You're a bunch of chemical reactions and electrical impulses. You're not any better than your pet dog or cat. Life has no meaning or purpose. Some day you will die, and when your life ends you will be extinguished or annihilated. You will go out of existence. Your body goes back to the earth, and your mind and life accomplishments come to nothing. So, life is birth, pain, pleasure, struggle, and death." (Charlie Liebert 1995)

Now you know why self-esteem is a big problem and teen suicide continues to increase. When I talk to teens that believe this, I have heard again and again, "Why keep living if life is so hopeless?" The Bible says you reap what you sow. If we sow hopelessness, what shall we reap? Contrast this with the Christian view!

"You are made in God's image. God's incredible design marvelously constructs your body. *But* you are separated from God by you own sin and rebellion. God has provided a way to return to him through Jesus Christ. When you die, you go to be with him forever, or you eternally perish in Hell. Your life does not end! This life is birth, pain, pleasure, and struggle, but death is defeated at the cross by Jesus. The best is yet to come, eternal life in Christ." (Charlie Liebert 1995)

The differences between the creation and evolution views are polar! They are as opposite as you can get! I know some readers will not accept this contrast, so let me substantiate it with quotes from evolutionists.

Nobel Laureate Francis Crick in his book, *The Astonishing Hypothesis,* said: "... you, your joys, and your sorrows, your memories and your ambitions, your sense of personal identity and free will, are in fact no more than the behavior of a vast assembly of nerve cells and their associated molecules. As Lewis Carroll's Alice might have phrased it: 'You're nothing but a pack of neurons.' This hypothesis is so alien to the ideas of most people alive today that it can truly be called astonishing."

Scientific American, in an article about Social Darwinists, said: "Darwinian science inevitably will and should have legal, political, and moral consequences. Some of the most pressing issues of the 90s, abortion, birth control, sexual discrimination, homosexuality, are in Darwin's beat. Yes, we are all animals descended from a vast lineage of replicators sprung from primordial pond scum."

Jeffery Dahmer, a serial murderer, was interviewed on *NBC Dateline.* When asked why he did what he did, said: "If a person doesn't think there is a God to be accountable to, then what's the point of trying to modify your behavior to keep within acceptable ranges? That's how I thought anyway. I always believed the theory of evolution as truth that we all just came from slime, pond scum. When we died, there is nothing. I've since come to believe the Lord Jesus Christ is truly God, and I believe that I as well as everyone else will be accountable to him."

Note: Yes, God saves the unworthy, but then who is worthy? There's none righteous; no, not *one!* All have gone astray! All have turned to their own way and God's condemnation is on *all* humanity!

Nobel Laureate Francis Crick proposed: "No newborn infant should be declared human until it has passed certain tests regarding its genetic endowment. If it fails these tests, it forfeits the right to live." Reported by Cal Thomas, *LA Times* Syndicate.

Former Colorado Gov. Lamm: "The elderly has 'a duty to die and get out of the way' and not tie up medical resources that could be used to benefit those with longer lives to live." Reported by Cal Thomas, *LA Times*.

Former Colorado Gov. Lamm: "They [the elderly] should emulate leaves of the season that 'fall off a tree forming humus for the other plants to grow.'" Reported by Cal Thomas, *LA Times*.

Are we then doomed? *No!* Our hope is for God to bring revival. But that would only be temporary. Our real hope is in the salvation that is in Jesus. Fight the good fight! Run the race! Finish well!

Here's a scenario I use when I teach youth seminars on Christian Apologetics. "There was great prosperity in Israel. Times were great. Those unpopular prophets, like Isaiah, had been warning of impending doom for a long time, but who believed them? If you want to see "political correctness" applied to one of God's prophets, read the book of Jeremiah. His whole life, as he lives it for God, is one disaster after another! Suddenly in those best of times, in one day, the ten tribes of Israel are carried off by the Assyrians. Isaiah was right! Put your faith in Christ and Christ alone. God's purpose *will* be worked out in history; after all, it is His Story! The world continues to live day by day, not remembering the lessons of history." (Charlie Liebert, 1998)

"What experience and history teach is this: that people and governments have never learned anything from history or acted on principles deduced from it." George Wilhelm Freidrich Hegel in *Philosophy of History.*

"Those who do not remember the past are condemned to relive it." George Santayana

The Apostle Peter wrote of these last days:

"And saying, where is the promise of his coming? For since the fathers fell asleep, **all things continue** as they were from the beginning of the creation." (2 Peter 3:4)

Another aspect of our value as humans is the way our bodies are constructed. We are "wonderfully and marvelously made." Today we know more about humans than ever before.

➤ A zygote, the fertilized egg in a woman's body, contains all the information for a full-grown adult. Nothing needs to be added.

➤ That one cell is a living human being!

➤ Man has twenty-three pairs of chromosomes filled with DNA.

➤ The DNA molecule, double helix, contains the genetic code that is:

- o Billions of atoms arranged in unique order for each person.
- o Writing out this code would fill six hundred books of a thousand pages each.
- o All of which is contained on a pinpoint.

And according to Evolution *It all happened by accident*!

Part 1. Death NOT Expected.
Chapter 3. Stephen A. Brown.

Stephen A. Brown 3/18/2017

I have known the Brown Family for more than 30 years. Parents, Scot, and Cindie, have four sons. They are unique in the many families we have known because Cindie has been blind since her youth. Yet she educated all four sons by home schooling. As Christians, Terry and I have worked, fellowshipped, prayed and studied Scripture with Scot and Cindie. They are two of the strongest believers we know. In 2022, two of the four sons were married with families.

The story told here is the life of their third born son, Stephen. It is included because it illustrates how a Christian father and mother dealt with a child controlled by his own sin. Stephen's life tells of a believer, coming to Jesus at age 9, then later, wandering into deep sin as a prodigal son. He goes into addictions of tobacco, alcohol, and drugs, and falls into the behaviors of the "gay" lifestyle. At 33, Stephen comes to repentance giving up the "gay" life and returns to the body of Christ in the church. Still battling heroine, he seeks a cure for this severe physical addiction.

You'll see an amazing person battle much of the powers of darkness. I predict you'll cry with joy but then sadness as his story ends. Most of all, you'll see how Christian parents deal with their wandering son. They didn't disown him. They didn't throw him out. They didn't discard his life. THEY LOVED him and did not give up believing he belonged to God. They truly understood God's covenant for our children and lived it out before all of us. Cindie's prayer makes this author cry every time I read it!

"Now look here, you ole devil. I was with Stephen when he was nine years old, and he confessed Jesus as his Savior. He is a child of the King, not your child.

So, get your lying, stealing, killing, destroying hands off him, and go back to HELL, where you belong.

Besides, Jesus is bigger and stronger than you. He has 2/3 of the angels, and you only have 1/3. So there, In Jesus' Name. Amen."

Biblical Background.

Before reading Cindie's *"Remembering Stephen"* you'll read the penalty for a rebellious child from Deuteronomy and the story of the

Prodigal son from the Gospel of Luke. This comparison illustrates the Old Covenant "under law," also called "The Covenant of Works" vs. the New Covenant "under grace," "The Gospel of Jesus Christ."

Before we read the Prodigal Son here is the Old Testament law regarding a rebellious child. Since rebellion is sin, <u>under the Law, it brings the penalty of death</u>. In the prodigal story the son returns to his father and receives restoration, grace, and new life. <u>Grace brings the reward of new life in Christ.</u>

A Rebellious Son - Deuteronomy 21:18–21

If a man has a stubborn and rebellious son who will not obey the voice of his father or the voice of his mother, and, though they discipline him, will not listen to them, then his father and his mother shall take hold of him and bring him out to the elders of his city at the gate of the place where he lives, and they shall say to the elders of his city, "This our son is stubborn and rebellious; he will not obey our voice; he is a glutton and a drunkard." Then all the men of the city shall stone him to death with stones. So, you shall purge the evil from your midst, and all Israel shall hear, and fear.

The Prodigal Son Luke 15:11-23.

Then Jesus said, "There was a man who had two sons. The younger son said to him, 'Father, give me my share of the estate.' So, he divided his property between them.

After a few days, the younger son got everything together and journeyed to a distant country, where he squandered his wealth in wild living.

After he had spent all, he had, a severe famine swept through that country, and he began to be in need. So, he went and hired himself out to a citizen of that country, who sent him into his fields to feed

51

the pigs. He longed to fill his belly with the pods the pigs were eating, but no one would give him a thing.

Finally, he came to his senses and said, "How many of my father's hired servants have plenty of food? But here I am, starving to death! I will get up and go back to my father and say to him, 'Father, I have sinned against heaven and against you. I am no longer worthy to be called your son. Make me like one of your hired servants."'

So, he got up and went to his father. But while he was still in the distance, his father saw him and was filled with compassion. He ran to his son, embraced him, and kissed him.

The son declared, 'Father, I have sinned against heaven and against you. I am no longer worthy to be called your son.'

But the father said to his servants, 'Quick! Bring the best robe and put it on him. Put a ring on his finger and sandals on his feet. Bring the fattened calf and kill it. Let us feast and celebrate. <u>For this son of mine was dead and is alive again! He was lost and is found!</u>'

Conclusion: The law in the Old Testaments brings justice, condemnation, and death, while the New Testament tells us of Jesus sacrifice for us that brings, grace, mercy, and life. Under the Law, we will perish in Hell. Under Grace, we will thrive in Heaven.

Old Testament Covenant, Works:
Moral Law brings justice and death.

New Testament Covenant, Grace:
Faith brings mercy and life.

Remembering Stephen, by Cindie Brown.

This is the life story of Stephen A. Brown as told by his mother, Cindie, who has been blind since she was thirteen. Scot Brown and Charlie Liebert assisted Cindie in her work as an Author. This Chapter was conceived on March 19, 2022, five years after Stephen's deadly accidental overdose of Heroin laced with Fentanyl. It is also published as a stand-alone, full color book with added pictures and is available on Amazon.com.

This is the life story of Stephen A. Brown as told by his mother Cindie.

Remembering Stephen

21st Century Prodigal Son

STEPHEN A. BROWN
JULY 2, 1982
MAR 19, 2017
FREE AT LAST

Written by Cindie Brown
with Scot Brown and Charlie Liebert

My name is Cindie Brown. I was six months old when I was told that I would be blind for life. My eyes were normal at birth, but unregulated oxygen in the incubator damaged them. I still had travel vision until I was almost 13. I'm married to my remarkable husband, Scot, and we have four sons: Aaron, Nathan, Stephen, and Zachery. In 2022, when this book was written, two of our sons were married and have their own families. This is the story of one son that did not marry but chose another path. All our family were raised as Christians, including Stephen. Here is his story!

Our 3rd son, Stephen, arrived at 4:54 p.m. on Friday, July 2, 1982. He was a very compliant baby, and he was the most straightforward pregnancy and delivery of our four boys.

When he was 13 months old, he began talking in complete sentences. We had some amusing and exciting conversations. As soon as he could walk, Stephen would take my hand because I'm blind and lead me into the yard, where he would describe to me a pretty leaf or unusual flower. Sometimes he would describe the colors of the sky. Stephen called days where the sun went in and out peek-a-boo days. That is what I still refer to them as today.

When Stephen was two years old, our pastor's wife, Margaret McKeever, taught his Sunday school class. Stephen had a tremendous crush on Miss Margaret. One morning, as he sat having a snack with me in the kitchen, he blurted out, "Mommy, I really love Miss Margaret, and someday when I am big, I will marry her." "Stephen, what about Dr. Joe, Miss Margaret's husband? Don't you think he might have something to say about all this?" Stephen sat silently pondering all this for some moments and then said, "Oh, Mom, it's okay. By the time I am big enough to marry Miss Margaret and take care of her, Dr. Joe will be so old and worn out that we can just give him away or put him in the trash." Next week at the church supper, I related this incident to Margaret, and she laughed so hard she cried. I told her that Dr. Joe better be sweet to her, for he had some stiff competition for her affections. I could hear her laughing all the way across the fellowship hall.

Authors Note by Cindie: I just found this "crush" incident written years ago and thought it was so funny I would include it. Many of our friends will know the ones involved in this incident, and I pray it might bring a lot of laughs to many hearts.

When Stephen was three, we had a large sleet storm. Scot (his father, my husband) wore heavy tall military boots during the storm. Stephen stepped into them and began to stomp around the house. They came nearly to his waist and looked hilarious. We all laughed so hard our sides hurt.

Stephen could make funny faces and imitate anything and anyone. He kept us in stitches each time he would impersonate anyone. Like other kids, he sometimes was in a bad mood or lost his temper, but he was usually cheerful and fun-loving.

Stephen started kindergarten at age five, but soon we brought him home to homeschool him with his two older brothers, Aaron, and Nathan. His youngest brother, Zachary, was born on June 11, just shy of Stephen's 6th birthday. Stephen spent a lot of time playing with Zac and reading to him over the years. Before Zac started school, Stephen read him all the C.S. Lewis Chronicles of Narnia books, Stephen was a very expressive reader. He used different voices for all the characters.

Though Stephen and Zac got along well, his older brothers and other boys often bullied Stephen. He would come into the house and watch longingly out the window at the boys in the backyard. Scot and I would find out later that this behavior is characteristic of boys who would later be homosexual. At this time, Scot and I were woefully ignorant of this fact.

The church has always been a large part of our family life. On January 6, 1992, at nine years old, Stephen came into my bedroom and asked to talk with me. He told me that he was ready to become a Christian. We had a long conversation about Jesus and what he had done for us by coming down from heaven as a baby and living a perfect life. We talked about His death on the cross as payment for sins and His remarkable resurrection. It was such a special privilege to lead my child in the sinner's prayer and pray with him for his salvation. I told him that he had made the most critical decision of his life. We found his Bible and wrote the date in big red letters on its front.

As Stephen grew into a teenager, he began to work in his dad's insurance office doing paperwork. He also received a job opportunity from Charlie Liebert, a contributor and publisher of this story, to work in Creation workshops and seminars. Charlie began taking him on road trips through North Carolina and surrounding states to do book fairs, workshops, and seminars selling homeschooling curricula and programs. Some of these programs were set up by Ken Ham's ministry, Answers in Genesis. These trips provided Stephen friendship with Charlie, opportunities to see unknown parts of the country, fascinating Bible discussions (about Creation and other spiritual matters), and much-needed income.

Contributor (Charlie Liebert) Commentary:

I'm interrupting Cindie's narrative to insert two incidents I had while traveling with Stephen when he worked as my assistant leading workshops & seminars for Ken Ham's Answers in Genesis.

Answers in Genesis scheduled a Homeschool graduation ceremony in Columbia, South Carolina, which included a three-hour Creation, Dinosaurs, and the Flood (CDEF) workshop for Grammar students on Friday Morning. This was Stephen's second trip with me. The first was a one-day trip to Winston-Salem for a two-hour evening seminar. In Columbia, Friday night, we had a Youth Talk Back Session for Middle and High School youth scheduled from 6:00-9:00 pm. We started with pizza at six. I gave a half-hour presentation on Creation that ended at 7:15. I asked for questions and started with two of my own questions: 1) Where did Cain's wife come from? 2) Was Noah's flood worldwide? It took about 10 minutes to answer those first two. There was a 10-second pause, and then the questions from the youth started flowing. Once the students realized I was giving reasonable, straightforward answers, the flood gates opened. At 9:15, the youth pastor was ready to close the session and asked for one more question. The question was "When does life begin?" I said to the pastor, "This may take some time." He gave me a "go ahead" nod. The discussion got very lively for more than an hour. The parents made us stop at 10:30 over the objection of most of the students. On our trip home, that evening, from Columbia, SC, to Greensboro, NC, Stephen, and I talked about Christian Apologetics. During the youth program, I shared an incident I had in a local high school related to life's conception. Stephen asked, "If God designed sex to conceive children, why do people do so many other things with sex?" I was surprised by the question and hesitated for several seconds. I decided not to go any further with this discussion. I said, "Stephen, many things God made are used by men in sinful ways. Sex is one of parts of his design for life that is most often used for behavior that breaks his commandments." Later, when I heard Stephen went into the "gay" lifestyle, I reflected on this, "Could I have done more in this dialogue?"

This incident was the beginning of my answering his questions on our travels. I loved those times because, besides my teaching him, I was forced to seek answers to questions I had never thought of myself. His creativity in asking questions was very challenging. We had more than 200 hours of Apologetics discussions during the time he worked with me.

The other incident with Stephen I want to share is a Creation Weekend program we did together in Southern Virginia. We did a Saturday workshop and seminar. On Sunday, I preached twice. The first service was contemporary from 8:00 to 10:15, and the second was traditional from 10:30 to 12:00. The first service started with a 50s-style rock band playing "What a Friend We Have in Jesus" with three verses in four different styles: Rock and Roll, Caribbean, Big Band, and New Orleans style. Twelve times altogether. Stephen sat mesmerized and told me he thought that it was AMAZING!

The pastor asked me to pick the invitation hymn at the end of the sermon. I decided, "It Is Well with My Soul." I used part of the third verse as the invitation.

> **My sin, oh, the bliss of this glorious thought**
> **My sin, not in part but the whole,**
> **Is nailed to the cross, and I bear it no more,**
> **Praise the Lord, praise the Lord, o my soul**
> It is well (it is well)
> With my soul (with my soul)
> It is well; it is well with my soul

On our two-hour trip back to Greensboro, Stephen and I used that song's verse to talk about theology and God's amazing grace. After this discussion, I would use these lines from that hymn as closing lines when giving my testimony.

Thank you, Stephen, for helping me make that decision. I loved our time together. Scot and Cindie, you were blessed to have had him as a son.

End of Contributor Commentary.

Resume Cindie's Narration.

Stephen seated, Nathan, Aaron, and Zachary.

Stephen never struggled with belief in Evolution from the time of these trips. When Stephen turned 16, Charlie blessed him again, giving him a Nissan truck with a camper top for his first vehicle. Stephen was so proud of his truck. It had lots of miles on it but ran well and was very special to him. Stephen would make lists of errands and run around town in his truck for the family.

My first real disappointment with Stephen occurred just after he turned 18. I was in the laundry room transferring clothes from the washer to the dryer when I dropped some clothes in the narrow spot beside the dryer. I noticed a jar and when I opened it, I discovered it filled with cigarette butts and water. I knew then that Stephen had been sneaking around smoking. Stephen was honest when I confronted him, but this became his first serious addiction.

In the months following, I received phone calls from men asking for Stephen. They had unfamiliar names and voices. When I questioned Stephen about them, he told me that they were friends he had met while out doing errands.

At first, I accepted his answer, but I became more uneasy and suspicious. I kept hearing Kevin and Richard's names more and more. On March 24, 2001, we had an extensive discussion, and it came out that Kevin and Richard were gay, and so was Stephen. Finally, the truth was out. To say we were devastated and shocked was an understatement. We knew homosexuality existed, but we never expected it to invade our family suddenly in this way. We began reading, researching, and learning about this condition from that day forward. "Focus on the Family" ministry was especially helpful. They provided many resources and urged us to attend a special seminar they were conducting in Kansas City. Scot and I went.

Many of the facts presented at the seminar were very unpleasant to hear. Still, we gained strength and resolve by knowing we weren't the only Christian family dealing with these challenging issues. Knowing that Stephen was homosexual plunged me deep into the Scriptures, searching for words of hope and relief. This was one of the beneficial aspects of this problem. Many nights I would awaken from a sound sleep and would know that Stephen was in trouble or that he needed protection.

Sometimes I would lie in bed and pray to myself very softly, but most of the time, I would rise, gather my Bibles to pray, and search for more words of encouragement. Many nights I prayed all night. This whole thing was exhausting. Talking with the Lord was the only way I could find peace and comfort. It was as if I had a lifeline in my hand and holding onto it was the only means of survival.

When he left our home to stay with Kevin and Richard, he anticipated friendly reception and amiability. Instead, he found male predators. They imprisoned him in their home, taking his money and car keys and enslaving him. He was required to do laundry, cleaning, cooking, and anything else they set for him to do. If he did not comply, he was punished. He was beaten, raped, and exposed to drugs. I don't know if all the boys knew these living conditions, but Aaron, our oldest son, did and withheld this information from me until after Stephen died, for he felt it was too painful for me to endure at the time it was happening.

Somehow, by the grace of God, Stephen escaped, and by the time I saw him again he had his car and all his personal possessions. You'd think suffering this kind of abuse would make one pause and consider withdrawing from the gay lifestyle, but that didn't happen. Maybe Stephen was young enough and optimistic enough to believe that he would eventually find a kindhearted partner who would care for him. Praise God for his escape from these two predators.

One of my most challenging tasks that summer was explaining to Zachary, Stephen's younger brother, what was involved in homosexuality and homosexual activities. I prayed for hours over the words to explain this, but to say he was shocked was an understatement. He tried hard to be a good brother to Stephen. I only saw one unkind interchange between them in all the years we dealt with these problems. We were all coping in our ways, trying to love our hurting family members as we ate together as a family. Nothing was easy, and things would get much more complicated before they got better.

As I have said, sometimes, I prayed quietly, but at other times my prayers went something like this:

> "Now look here, you ole Devil. I was with Stephen when he was nine years old, and he confessed to Jesus as his Savior.
>
> He is a child of the King, not your child. So, get your lying, stealing, killing, destroying hands off him, and go back to HELL, where you belong.
>
> Besides, Jesus is bigger and stronger than you. He has 2/3 of the angels, and you only have 1/3.
>
> So there, In Jesus' Name. Amen."

Publishers Note by Charlie Liebert. When I read about Cindie's prayer I was reminded of Monica, Saint Augustine's mother who prayed for him for years. MOTHERS: PRAY FOR YOUR SONS!!

That probably wasn't exactly what I should have prayed, but I did it many times anyway. Usually, I would feel much better afterward.

We learned that Stephen attended a gay pride event with his friends in Washington D.C. I shuddered as I contemplated all the acting out that could accompany such an event. Later he tearfully confessed to me that he was taking free drugs from the Health Department for a condition he had contracted from that event. I had to go and find a private place to have a good cry. It was so very sad.

In April 2001, Stephen moved in with his older brother, Aaron, and worked for him in his landscaping business. In June, Stephen went to Virginia to visit with another gay friend he knew. That situation became intolerable, and in about two weeks, he called to ask if he could come back home for a while. We picked him up from Virginia the first weekend of July. Immediately he found a job in a grocery store and began taking classes at a community college to obtain his GED.

We gave Stephen a key to Scot's office. This enabled him to do paperwork for Scot whenever his schedule permitted. In early 2001, Stephen entered Scot's office and used the facility for a sexual encounter. He knew this was a blatant abuse of the privilege we had extended to him. As a result, we further insisted that his friends could only be in our home when we were at home.

Stephen maintained that he and his friends could and should have access to our home even when we were not present. So, after supper on Thursday, September 27, 2001, he simply drove off in a huff and lived for a few months out of his car.

Despite his difficulties and the brokenness and darkness in his life, he never seemed hardened or embittered. He always retained a conscience and a heart. He seemed sad when he did and said things that caused us pain. He showed gratitude for almost anything we gave or provided to him.

For the next two months, we'd see his battered car in the driveway where he had slept. We would invite him in for breakfast. He would usually eat, visit, then rest awhile and be on his way again.

One Sunday in late October, he knocked on the door and asked to come in. "Mom," he said, "I am so hungry I could eat dirt. Do you think we could have something to eat and then rest for a while?" Though our visit was pleasant, my heart was broken. I knew he was suffering, and it was hard to watch. His dad had taken teenagers from church on a long hike so he wouldn't be home until early evening.

When he left, hours later, I gave him another lunch I'd made and a big handful of change to put gas in his car. It was all I could do to let him go on his way. I wept for our son! The darkness of sin seemed to overwhelm me.

In 2001, Stephen came for my birthday armed with a greeting card and a bag of candy I liked. He told me that he would soon be moving in with a new friend that I'll call Andrew. Stephen had answered an ad for a guy that needed a roommate. This relationship would last seven years until the fall of 2008. Before it ended, they would buy and remodel a small house together and even take a vacation to Jamaica.

Two of the first things those two guys did were to join a volleyball team and a bowling league. They often rode their roller blades together through local parks. After brief periods of employment as a receptionist at Red Roof Inn and as a security officer at a small company, he enrolled at Leon's School of Cosmetology in Greensboro. Stephen performed well during his year-long course of study. Scot and I often went there for Stephen to practice on us with perms, haircuts, etc. This was a path I long suspected he might take. As a small boy, he would kneel on the bed behind me and fashion my long hair into various hairdos. I loved to see the different hairstyles, and it gave us time to be with him, share and have a few laughs.

Stephen graduated from cosmetology school in the summer of 2003. He got his first job, bought his supplies, and began developing a large loyal clientele. They followed him faithfully from salon to salon as he traveled to different positions around Greensboro. He was often inundated with money and gifts around his birthday and Christmas. Many men and women wouldn't let anyone, but Stephen touch their hair or face. Their generosity to him was incredible.

Because he was able to work as a hairdresser until shortly before his death, he had financial resources. He never ransacked our home or stole money or property to fuel his drug habit.

That summer, Stephen turned 21 on July 2, 2002. He took a drink to celebrate his birthday and the awfulness of alcoholism closed tight on his life like a trap. He would eventually get free from it, but it took quite a toll on every significant relationship of his life and his physical and emotional health. The first time we were officially invited to Stephen and Andrew's home was October 5 for Andrew's birthday. Scot and I purchased him a lovely leather Bible with his name engraved on it. Each day I would hold the book and fervently pray that Andrew would read the precious Word and find true salvation. He seemed very touched when he received it, but whether he read it, I do not know.

When we arrived at their home for the party, we found the house fully decorated with streamers, balloons, and banners. Stephen made a massive pan of Oreo dirt cake, Andrew's favorite, and a layer cake with chocolate frosting. Before the cakes were served, one of the guys spoke up and said, "Stephen, serve the real lady's cake first." This broke the tension. We all doubled over with laughter, then we relaxed and just had fun.

As we became acquainted with Stephen and Andrew as a couple, we learned that Andrew was the son of an American G.I. and a Vietnamese mom. Under these circumstances in Vietnam, Vietnamese American racially mixed children were not treated well. When Andrew was between 5 and 6 years old, a group of nuns escorted several of these kids from their home's remote villages to the capital city Saigon. Viet Cong guerrillas harassed and chased them all the way to their destination, burning everything around them. The children barely made it onto planes leaving the country before communism took over. They flew to America, where they were adopted. Andrew was taken in by a military family and had adopted brothers and sisters. Even as an adult, he still had terrible nightmares about his escape from Vietnam.

As our family walked through these tough times and dealt with Stephen's problems of homosexuality, drugs, drama, and alcoholism, some members of our family became so uncomfortable that they didn't feel they could spend significant holidays with Stephen. This saddened me, but I realized that I had to consider every family member's emotion and be as loving, flexible, and supportive as possible. Sometimes it felt like I was walking a tight rope, but God upheld me through it all. Scot and I knew that we had to make small holiday celebrations as fun and meaningful as the larger ones. I would pull out China and crystal, cook favorite dishes for the 3 or 4 of us, plan things like walks, movies, or games, and enjoy it all.

One year we had three different Christmas gatherings. During our 1st, Scot and I celebrated with his mom and Stephen and his partner, Michael. Two days later, we celebrated with Nathan and his family. The following day we drove to VA., where we had Christmas with Aaron and his family.

Stephen improved their circumstances somewhat by purchasing an excellent Honda Civic. This gave them reliable transportation. He also found a puppy and rescued him. This dog became a companion for Andrews's German Shepherd, Anja. Eli, Stephen's new dog, lived with him until 2014 and brought him hours of companionship. Unfortunately, he had to be put to sleep when he contracted cancer. It was sad for them both.

In 2004, Stephen entered the world of drag. He began doing makeovers for the contestants in drag competitions. He also did a makeover for his older brother, Aaron, for something called "The Womanless Beauty Contest." Somewhere we have amazing pictures of Aaron as a woman. After the event, he met one of his friends, Adam, who freaked out when he saw Aaron as a girl.

Aaron, Nathan, Stephen, and Zachary

When Andrew and Stephen broke up, Stephen moved into a small apartment alone with his dog. He lived there until the summer of 2010. Early on the morning of July 24, Scot got a call from Stephen. He had been drinking and driving and was arrested. He fled first from the officer but then slowed down and came to a stop. As a result, Scot had to go downtown to pick him up. He received a suspended sentence of two years and served ten weekends in jail. He lost a lot of his rights as a citizen. He was in the process of getting his license and rights back when he died. He came to live with us at the end of 2010.

Stephen also attended rehab classes and AA (Alcoholics Anonymous) meetings. Scot and I attended many of his meetings with him for support. While visiting me one day, we started talking about his experiences. He said they had to go around the circle telling their names and saying what their problem substances were. One guy gave his name and said he dealt with alcohol. Another said his name and said he dealt with marijuana. Stephen said he was thinking, "I am Stephen, and what haven't I tried." I asked if he had tried meth. He said, "Only once, but I will never do it again. It was the most horrible thing I have done."

Leaving him in jail for the first time was awful for Scot and me. A guard at the prison found out that Stephen loved to cook. So, he arranged to have Stephen spend most of his time in the kitchen. This way, he could avoid the more brutal inmates and be safer. He cooked and scoured the whole kitchen and cafeteria. It was God's way of protecting him from men who might have harmed him.

Because of his DUI, Stephen couldn't drive a car, so he purchased a scooter called his Liquor-cycle. It was red. This was his method of transportation until his death. He especially disliked traveling on it in the extreme cold of Winter. After Stephen died, we kept his helmet and jacket in case Scot wanted to get a dirt bike for entertainment.

Stephen spent Christmas day with Scot, me, and our youngest son Zachery. We had breakfast and then opened our gifts. It began to snow later in the morning, and we had heavy snow by evening. Our time together was beautiful. We all helped to prepare the Christmas dinner. Later in the day, we made a trip through the snow to see our newborn 8th grandchild. He was named Grayson. He was a special

Christmas blessing. That night we went for a long walk in the snow. We used our sleds, let the snow spray in our faces, and had fun together. Then we headed home for dessert and a warm-up. We all felt so blessed. None of us foresaw the hard times that were ahead.

We invited Stephen to have lunch with us during the snowy week after Christmas. When we picked him up, he showed us a beautiful scarf a client had knitted for him. It was a lovely shade of purple and made from soft cotton yarn. As we retraced our steps to the car after a pleasant meal, he spied a homeless man in ragged clothes on a bench. Without a word, he unfastened the new scarf and, bending down, gently draped it around the man's neck and shoulders. I said, "Stephen, your new pretty scarf." when we were out of earshot.

"O, Mom, it's okay. He needed it so much more than I did." That was Stephen, all right. He was such a giver. He freely gave what he had and never looked back.

Things rocked along a few weeks in a typical fashion. In February, our new grandson developed a severe case of a virus called RSV and had to be hospitalized. Scot and I had to go to their home and stay with them for a few days. Stephen came with us and was so much help to us. The kids were very upset about their brother being sick and missing their parents so much that they were reluctant and stubborn about cooperating with anything. Stephen showed them funny things on his phone, made funny faces, and did all kinds of things to distract them and get them to cooperate. Before we knew it, he had them laughing. He helped feed them their meals, bathed them, and read to them before they went to bed. I don't know what we would have done without his help.

In August 2011, Stephen began to live with a guy I will call Michael. He claimed to have some disability, but he looked normal to us. He did not work, and Stephen paid for all expenses. Scot and I both disliked him at once. We did our best to get along with him but warned Stephen to get away from him as fast as possible. We had Michael in our home several times. Once, he brought a delicious cheesecake he had made. He was still obnoxious, and I found it hard to tolerate him.

Once when Stephen did or said something Michael disliked, he went to the cabinet when Stephen was away and smashed eight place settings of crystal and China that Stephen had received as a gift from my parents. Stephen was broken-hearted about this, and so were we.

Stephen finally ended the relationship around my birthday in November of 2014. Once more, he lived with us and would be with us until he passed away. We spent a wonderful Christmas with the whole family. Stephen and I baked and decorated together just as we had when he was growing up. In January, he began attending church with us. The first sermon was on David and Goliath. Our pastor shot an orange ping pong ball across the sanctuary with a sling from the Holy Land and Stephen caught it. The pastor asked two questions in this sermon 1. What giants in your lives do you need to slay? 2. What things in your lives do you need to change to be right with God so that God can help you slay your giants? I believe those questions were used by the Holy Spirit to begin to draw Stephen back to God. We found that ball in his mementos after his death.

He made friends quickly and soon started greeting at the door and helping to make coffee on Sunday mornings. He gravitated to the ones on the fringes of the church. Often, we would see him in earnest conversation with a teen he knew to be hurting or in trouble. If a homeless guy walked in, Stephen was at his side, making him feel welcome.

It was in Sunday school that I was most surprised. He began to participate in discussions about the scriptures actively. I was amazed at the insights he made about the Bible lessons. He had been listening to the Word being preached at church, and his seeking to grow from it was beautiful to watch. I believe some of this foundation was from the many hours he spent traveling with Charlie Liebert.

At home, we did yard work and errands together. He often went to stores with us and helped put groceries away. Once a week or so, he would find a recipe he liked and even fix dinner for us. One of my favorite times was being with him after dinner. We would go out to the carport so he could have a smoke. He would again describe the sky or tell me about the birds and animals nearby. His favorite thing was to watch the sunset and the clouds when rain was coming.

Late at night, he would go out on the front porch and watch for stars. There was a fox that prowled in our bushes at night. At first, Stephen's presence startled the animal, but as he continued to come out at night, he would find the fox seemed to be waiting for his arrival. He would talk to the fox as if he understood him. It was kind of cool.

Still, there were periods of moodiness, and occasionally I could hear him getting sick in the bathroom. I thought it was just stress, but it was more than that. He had contracted AIDs and was using heroin to cover the pain. Stephen was humiliated and he did not yet want to share everything with us. As the weeks went by, he grew sicker, and we knew something more was wrong. It all came out in the fall of 2015.

He was hospitalized under the care of an infectious disease doctor. He had to take two medications that cost more than $6000 each a month. Once when he opened his medicines, he noticed that the Trump Foundation paid for them, and he mentioned this to me. We were both thankful and surprised by this fact. The man who wanted to be our President was helping him stay alive. Hardest of all, as we talked, we began to cry through complex issues and the many misunderstandings of the past.

We gave him a Geneva study Bible, and from his daily questioning, we knew he was reading it. He brought the Bible to me one day and pointed out I Corinthians 6, verses 11, 15, and 16.

11 And such were some of you. But you were washed, sanctified, and justified in the name of the Lord Jesus Christ and by the Spirit of our God... 15 Do you not know that your bodies are members of Christ? Shall I then take the members of Christ and make them members of a prostitute? Never! 16 Or do you not know that he who is joined to a prostitute becomes one body with her? As it is written, "The two will become one flesh.

When he got to verse 11 and read the words "and such were some of you," He said, "I know I need to change, Mom, but it is so hard. I feel such shame." In a voice barely above a whisper, he said, "After all I've done, I can't see how Jesus would want anything to do with me." I enfolded him in my arms and began slowly to rock him back and forth as we had done when he was small. "Stephen, if God loved the people in Corinth and changed their hearts, He can do this for you. You only need to ask Him. He is with you and won't turn you away." We cried and hugged for a long time.

He further explained that if there were one other thing he could change, it would be to break his addictions. He explained that they made him feel like he was in quicksand and couldn't get free. He said it made him do and say things that hurt those he loved. He explained the words of the song "Hotel California." He told me he believed it

73

was a song about addiction. It said, "You can check out any time you like, but you can never leave." This was a day I would never forget.

Publishers Note: Here is a link to the Eagle's song Hotel California. https://www.youtube.com/watch?v=UehilhnMt5Y There is a of controversy about whether the lyrics deal with drug addiction. Make your own decision. It certainly portrays the power of drug addiction through its many descriptive pictures.

To help Stephen find a way to conquer his addictions we took him to meet a good friend and counselor, Dr. S. Stephen began working with him through his many issues in the next few days. Stephen was tested for drugs and the results showed heroin use. Dr. S recommended several good facilities where Stephen could go for help. Stephen picked a year long, Christian-based program called Freedom Farm. https://www.freedomfarmministries.org

We were hopeful because everything was set for him to enter the facility on Monday, March 20, 2017. On March 18, we drove to the mountains where Stephen participated in a wedding for friends. Our family came over for pizza and soda at home that night, and Stephen explained his plans. He shared a letter to our church family he had written to define the next steps of his life.

Dear Church Family,

My name is Stephen Brown, I may not know you by name, but you all know mine. I have been so touched by the Love and acceptance from everyone. My experience with organized Religion has been Rocky at best. God says, treat others the way you want to be treated. Not in the same words, and this is quite simplified. I feel you all embody this so much it has warmed my, sometimes Stuck in the mud, soul. You know, you have seen me sitting, looking like I lost my dog...but everyone always says, "Hi, how are you? Good to see you." All I want is for you all to know how much you all mean to me. And thank you from the bottom of my heart. I will be back in a year or so. I am taking some time to renew my faith in a faith-based, year-long program. I would love to correspond with anyone who wants. You can give your address to my mom and dad. See you in a year or so! Please pray for me.

Stephen Brown

On the morning of the 19th, Scot went to wake Stephen for church but didn't see him in his room. He walked around the bed and found him curled up on the floor. He had passed away. His body was still warm. He had taken one more dose of heroin and it contained fentanyl. When Scot came and told me to get dressed, I knew something was wrong. I remember standing in the middle of our room as Scot walked slowly toward me. He held me close and told me Stephen had passed away. The shock and grief were overwhelming. I heard the awful sound of Stephen's body being thrust into a body bag. The rest of the morning was a blur as emergency vehicles, family, and friends arrived in quick succession. It was awful. God began to carry us through our grief slowly. The Christian community began to shower us with food, visits, and an ocean of calls and cards that lasted for months. We had Stephen's wooden coffin made.

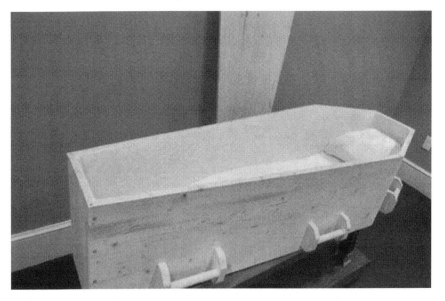

We buried our son, Stephen A. Brown, in a private family service on the 25th on our oldest son's property in the North Carolina mountains.

A memorial service was held along with a dinner and reception at our church on the 30th. Scot planned another event to honor our son. Scot dyed his hair bright pink in honor of Stephen. He didn't tell me he was doing this, which caused a stir at church. We stood with all our friends and received their hugs, tears, and laughter. We would have many hard days ahead of us. Some days were now much harder than others. Through all of this, we felt the love of our family and community, the love of God, and through His Word. The Holy Spirit kept reassuring us of his love and presence. We attended a support group for parents of overdose victims for almost two years. I would have 13 months of counseling where I could pour out my heart with a lovely believing friend. As we walked into the sanctuary with pink hair, we knew that Stephen was safe in the arms of His Savior and was smiling at us.

On Stephen's birthday, Sunday, July 2, 2018, we placed a simple granite marker on his grave early that morning.

Stephen was FREE AT LAST.

John 8:36. "If the Son shall make you free, you shall be free indeed."

Postscript by Cindie.

Four days after Stephen's passing, I had an encounter with the Holy Spirit that really helped give me peace. I had spent a sleepless night the night before, for I knew that we would be going to the funeral home to see Stephen's coffin delivered.

The grief and sadness were almost overwhelming. After breakfast, I lay down for a short nap. I awoke from a dream sometime later in a cold sweat. I had heard again in my mind the awful sound of Stephen's body being thrust into a body bag. I rolled up in a ball, sobbing so hard I thought I would suffocate. The Spirit spoke to me in an almost audible voice. "Cindie," He said, "My son died all alone on a cross so that when you lost your son, you would never be alone. I am Immanuel, and I am here with you, right here with you He repeated. A feeling of unexplainable peace stole over me, and I could relax and breathe again. I give thanks to God for His love and grace to me.

More than four years after Stephen's passing, on Christmas 2021, we were all together for a wonderful day and a half of visiting and fun. Things kicked off with a big turkey dinner with all the trimmings at our house. After dessert and cleanup, we all went to Nathan's, where we ran around and played or drove dirt bikes. At dusk, we met around our firepit. I led the family in singing Christmas carols and then we prayed with and for each other. It was one of the sweetest hours we have spent together in years. As the children sang and prayed, it brought tears to my eyes. It was wonderful to hear them thank Jesus for their many blessings and testify to their faith. Afterward, we went inside to open family gifts and have a supper of turkey sandwiches, chips, fruit, etc., and more dessert. It was truly a day to remember.

God is so good, and for now, life is well. We are still a family, walking through life's heartaches and joys and still finding ways to be together and enjoy each other's company. This summer, we have another family vacation at a lake near Charlotte for lots of swimming, boating, noise laughter, and family fun. Our first great-grandchild may be there. We will just have to wait and see.

Are we a perfect family? No, but we are still a family. Loving, praying, and walking through life together. I am so grateful that life is good for each member of this precious group. God is so good, and life is good as well.

For Stephen, Cindie Brown

Chapter 4. Grieving Death NOT Expected.

Mourning and grief are the topics in many books that give good advice of how to deal with these processes in the death of a loved one. Most cities in the US have counselors to help outline and lead you through the grieving process. I am not going to outline the normal grieving process here. There are substantial resources available, and it's been well done by many before me. WE are going MUCH DEEPER. When a person dies in a time that was anticipated from disease or the result of prior injuries, we grieve their loss. This book begins with the next step after this common grief, <u>death by sudden, unexpected events.</u> You have just read an example of that in *"Remembering Stephen."*

Five of the Six "W" Questions.

I'm going to use Dorothy Ellen Rose's death as the example, to develop the structure of the unexpected death grieving process because it was sudden, but by natural causes.

In all areas of human endeavor, particularly science, the six "W" questions are used to define the situation, Who, What, When, Where, How, and Why. Here is Dorothy's death by the six "W's

Who? Dorothy Ellen Rose.

What? Her Death.

Where? Amityville, New York.

When? 11/09/1960

How? Cerebral Hemorrhage.

Why? This question is not asked because either 1) the general answer is already known or 2) the question's answer is obvious – because they had a disease or accident.

The fall of humankind by Adam and Eve brought SIN and death to the Universe. The "Why" question is essentially answered for all believing Christians. Sin brought death! In the Garden of Eden before the fall there was NO death, but God said to ADAM.

Genesis2:16-17. And the LORD God commanded him, "You may eat freely from every tree of the garden, 17but you must not eat from the tree of the knowledge of good and evil; for in the day that you eat of it, you will surely die."

So, death entered the Universe because of Adam's sin. *I Corinthians 15:21 For since by man (Adam) came death...*

For the unbeliever to answer WHY a particular person died at that moment IS NOT KNOWABLE??? It could be bad luck, fate, accident, illness, etc. For the believer it is God's providential will and like our salvation known by Him before the foundation of the world.

At the next level, death by suicide, the Why question becomes central because his/her death was an act of human will and we want a reason, "WHY did they do it?" "WHY then?" "WHY that way?" WHY, WHY, WHY?"

The difference in the origin of death between atheism and Christianity is a great comfort for the Christian because we hope in God's promise to abolish death.

Biblical / Creation view of death: temporary and bad.
- **an intruder, caused by SIN**
- **not part of the biblical created order**
- **began at "The Fall." Genesis 3**
- **will have its end in the lake of fire. Revelation 20**
- **NOT in humankind's Creation. Genesis 1-2.**
- **NOT in humankind's destiny. Revelation 21-22.**

Death will go out of existence. If death is the way the Universe began, we are WITHOUT hope which is where evolution leaves us.

Evolution's view of death: permanent and good.
- An essential part of Evolution's creative force.
- Has always been here & will be until the end of time.

Comprehension.

When the bad news of a person's death comes to us our first reaction is not to believe it. In the case of Dorothy in1960 I asked the giver of the news to repeat what they said. Our intellectual understanding of what we heard lags our comprehension. I heard it, I didn't get it, I heard again now I understand but still don't get it. Part of our inability to grasp death is the origin of death itself. We know in our innermost being that death is not supposed to be part of the world. Yet it is. The origin of death goes back to how mankind came into existence. There are only two real possibilities. Life suddenly appeared through some miraculous series of event (Biblical Creation). Death was not part of the original Creation but is an intruder and will be destroyed at the end of time. The other possibility is life developed from preexisting material during very long periods of time (atheistic Evolution). Death is an essential part of Evolution, and it cannot move forward, nor will work without it.

Shock.

After about one week, I finally fully comprehended my loved one is dead. But I still don't want to believe it. This stage, shock, can also be called denial. This is a most common human reaction to deny what we know to be true but don't want it to be. It is one of the common behaviors of our sinful nature illustrated in Romans 1:19-22.

For what can be known about God is plain to them because God has shown it to them. For his invisible attributes, namely, his eternal power and divine nature, have been clearly perceived, ever since the creation of the world in the things that have been made. So, they are without excuse. For although they knew God, they did not honor him as God or give thanks to him, but they became futile in their thinking, and their foolish hearts were darkened. Claiming to be wise, they became fools,

This stage passes as we accept the person is dead. Now grief begins.

Grief.

Here is a definition of grief from the Mayo Clinic edited to only include grief from death, not grief from other sources:

"Grief is a strong, sometimes overwhelming emotion for people, that stems from the loss of a loved one. They might find themselves feeling numb and removed from daily life, unable to carry on with regular duties while saddled with their sense of loss.

Grief is the natural reaction to loss. Grief is both a universal and a personal experience. Individual experiences of grief vary and are influenced by the nature of the death of a loved one.

Experts advise those grieving to realize they can't control the process and to prepare for varying stages of grief. Understanding why they're suffering can help, as can talking to others and trying to resolve issues that cause significant emotional pain, such as feeling guilty for a loved one's death. Mourning can last for months or years. Generally, pain is tempered as time passes and as the bereaved adapts to life without a loved one." **END of Quote.**

The grieving process is normal. Consult health care professionals if you have questions. Outside help is sometimes beneficial to people trying to recover and adjust to a close person's death.

For an excellent article about the steps in the grieving process:
https://www.usurnsonline.com/grief-loss/grieving-process/

"If only?"

The last item we will consider in our grief at the "NOT expected" level is "IF Only" statements that analyze which events or circumstances which could have been changed in the past to prevent the death.

If you're uncertain about whether your mourning is subsiding, look at your speech. Is it not uplifting? IF we believe God is Sovereign and he ordains all events then "IF Only" questions deny our faith.

We are questioning if the situation of the death could have been changed to prevent the REAL outcome. This form of questioning may satisfy our emotions, but it is useless because we can't change the past. Here are examples of some "IF only's" I've asked when I heard of a sudden, unexpected death.

If only he'd seen the car coming.
If only they'd seen the truck hit the ice & start to jackknife.
If only the driver was not drunk.
If only the heroine had not been laced with fentanyl.
If she'd been closer to a hospital instead of…
If only they'd recognized the symptoms…
 If only…If only…If only…

This process of wishing to change the past is not only futile but questions our faith in God's sovereign purposes. Although this questioning is considered by many grief counselors as beneficial, as a Christian, I find it challenging to my faith and not uplifting. IF we believe God is Sovereign, then, He ordains all events. "IF Only" presses us to deny our faith.

Westminster Confession.

Here from the Westminster Confession Larger Catechism are two questions that relate to this.

Q. *12. What are the decrees of God?*

A. God's decrees are the wise, free, and holy acts of the counsel of his will, whereby, from all eternity, he hath, for his own glory, unchangeably foreordained whatsoever comes to pass in time, especially concerning angels and men.

Q. 18. *What are God's works of providence?*

A. God's works of providence are his most holy, wise, and powerful preserving and governing all his creatures, ordering them, and all their actions, to his own glory.

In Terry and my grieving, we both recognized that asking these "IF Only" of questions would tend to take us away from faith to rely on "unsolvable speculation". We developed a simple strategy. If either one of us began to go into this area the other one would call them out. When we talked about the past, if one went to "If only?" the other would say; "Don't go there!" Both of us said that many times in the early days after our grief began. Here is another therapy that helped me personally weep through my pain.

Charlie's Music Therapy.

I'm revealing here my "musical therapy" that was extremely helpful in the first weeks after I began mourning. It helped me to express my grief at anger at death, Satan and all his minions. When I woke up after midnight, I'd often feel the weight of death by suicide on my emotions. I'd pick up my iPhone, put in my ear buds in and play a series of songs and weep while they play. This usually went on for 30 to 45 minutes. Terry was usually sleeping because it was often at 1AM or 4 AM. As I moved from song to song, I wept for various aspects of the situation. As I list the pieces below, I'm including the topic of my weeping After I finished listening, I would go back to sleep with the "peace that passes understanding."

I know it sounds strange, but I start with **"Master of the House" from "Les Misérables."** WHY? Because I want to remember who I am. I am NOT MASTER OF THE HOUSE, but I thought I was when I was an atheist This video uses the LORD's name in vain and in some sense glorifies sin so if you are sensitive to my declaration as a willful sinner skip this video.

The Apostle Paul summarizes our history of sin and redemption in 1 Corinthians 6:9-11. I wasn't all those sinners listed, but I was quite a few of them.

Or do you not know that the unrighteous will not inherit the kingdom of God? Do not be deceived: neither the sexually immoral, nor idolaters, nor adulterers, nor men who practice homosexuality, nor thieves, nor the greedy, nor drunkards, nor revilers, nor swindlers will inherit the kingdom of God. And **such were some of you.** *But you were washed, you were sanctified, you were justified in the name of the Lord Jesus Christ and by the Spirit of our God.*

If you want to remember "such were some of you," listen to *Master of the House".*

Understanding who we are in relation to God is essential to a right understanding of who He is. In all three Synoptic Gospels Jesus said, *"I came not to call the righteous, but sinners to repentance." Matthew 9:13, Mark 2:17, Luke 5:32.* We must recognize we are lost sinners. Three of the most important leaders in the Bible, Moses,

King David, and The Apostle Paul were ALL murderers of the worse sort, killing by intent. I call this "calling of the 1st degree." In our justice system this is called murder in the first degree, and it carries the strongest punishment our culture allows the death penalty in many states.

First: Master of the House by Alun & Jenny. 5:44
Weep for: SORROW, our sin and my years lost as an atheist
https://www.youtube.com/watch?v=VALfpc-dJ7s

Second: "You Raise Me Up" BYU Vocal Point. 4:17
Weep for: SORROW, sudden, unexpected death
https://www.youtube.com/watch?v=rcLl0A-lXIc
When I am down and, oh my soul, so weary
When troubles come and my heart burdened be.
Then, I am still and wait here in the silence
Until You come and sit awhile with me.

Third: "I Know Who Holds Tomorrow." 4:21
Weep for: SORROW, thoughts of and death by suicide
https://www.youtube.com/watch?v=C7BtGs1w6hA
Many things about tomorrow
I don't seem to under understand
But I, I know, I know, I know who holds tomorrow
And I know who holds, who holds my hand

Note from the Petersens: Upon losing his wife at a young age, Ira Stanphill wrote "I Know Who Holds Tomorrow" expressing a prayer of surrender to his Savior under circumstances he didn't understand. God doesn't promise that walking with him will be easy, but what he does promise is that every day of our lives is in his hands, and we can rest in the hope of his Son, Jesus Christ, who paid the punishment for our sins so that we can have hope and eternity with him!

Fourth: "It Is Finished" Gaither Vocal Band. 6:06

Weep for: SORROW, the lost souls, outside Christ.

https://www.youtube.com/watch?v=ybU_ZK0rPeo

Now in my heart the battle was still raging
Not all prisoners of war had come home
These were battlefields of my own making
I didn't know that the war had been won
O' but then I heard that the king of the ages
He had fought all my battles just for me
And victory, victory was mine for the claiming*

And now praise his name, I'm free...
It is finished and Jesus is LORD!

* I know "claiming" is not a right word, but that's the lyrics

Fifth: "Amazing Grace, My Chains are Gone." 4:40

Weep for: JOY, salvation through Jesus' death /resurrection.

https://www.youtube.com/watch?v=Obp-9BEZe1c&list=RDObp-9BEZe1c&start_radio=1&rv=Obp-9BEZe1c&t=0

My chains are gone. I've been set free
My God, my Savior has ransomed me
And like a flood His mercy reigns
Unending love, amazing grace

Sixth: "Because He Lives" Celtic Worship. 5:19

Weep for: JOY, for God's promise of death's death!

e.g., Revelation 21-22, wipe away every tear.

https://www.youtube.com/watch?v=RFIr8-gH55E

And then one day, I'll cross that river

And fight life's final war with pain

And then, as death gives way to victory

I'll see the lights of glory and I'll know he lives

Because I know, I know he holds the future

Life is worth the living just because he lives.

Seventh: The Holy City, Jerusalem. 5:14

Weep for: JOY, your redemption draweth nigh!

https://www.youtube.com/watch?v=7BM9E1hEVrg

And once again the scene was changed,

New earth there seemed to be, I saw the Holy City

Beside the tideless sea, No need of moon or stars by night...

Or sun to shine by day, it was the new Jerusalem

That would not pass away, Jerusalem! Jerusalem

Sing for the night is o'er, Hosanna in the highest

Hosanna for evermore

Go to sleep with the peace that passes understanding.

Part 2. Death BY Suicide.

Shawn Woolley graduated from Osceola High School in May of 1998.

Chapter 5. Shawn by Liz Woolley.

Shawn's story is here because I worked with Liz and John of OLGA (On-Line Gamers Anonymous) publishing two books for them. His death was not in vain because his mom, Liz, founded this ministry that has freed many from addiction to video games. Visit https://www.olganon.org/home

Shawn: "Your Son Did Not Die in Vain!"

Every Mom has a mission. To love, guide and protect her family. Don't mess with her while she is on it. Vicki Reece

This is the true story of a mother's battle for her son's life against a video game??

On February 12, 2000, my son, Shawn Woolley, celebrated his 20th birthday. Shawn was living at my home at the time. Shawn took his birthday money and purchased his FIRST MMORPG (Massive Multiplayer Online Role-Playing Game) called Everquest. I thought it was just another computer game and so did he. However, this one decision radically altered Shawn's life and everyone around him. It was a tragic game-changer in Shawn's life.

How can one video game change a person's life forever? In this chapter, we will summarize Shawn's life. To know the complete story about Shawn, read the book "Your Son Did NOT Die in Vain" written by Liz Woolley with John M. Langel, Sr. Purchase from Amazon.com in color, black & white or eBook format.

Shawn Woolley was a sensitive person. He was not competitive athletically. Shawn enjoyed sports just for the fun of it. Shawn loved art and he was very good at it. He was quite creative with his art and writing. Shawn liked to do other activities like bowling, downhill snow skiing, roller skating, street hockey, and bike riding. Shawn played the saxophone and trumpet in the school and marching bands. He also liked going boating and fishing. Some of the computer games that Shawn liked to play were Doom, Doom II, Solitaire, Pacman, Cyberia, and Mortal Kombat II. Shawn was funny. Shawn liked to make people laugh. He just wanted people to like him.

Shawn had been playing off-line computer games for about the past ten years, with no significant character or social changes in his life. When Shawn was six years old, he was diagnosed with epilepsy. He had not had any seizures since he continued to take his medication as prescribed. The video games he had been playing was designed for fun and entertainment. Each game had a beginning and an end. They were not continuously advancing to new and higher levels which Everquest did.

The War Begins.
In 2000, life in the Woolley household drastically changed after Shawn's 20th birthday. A new force, a new video game, was now at play in his life. The battle began. Shawn became heavily involved with the virtual Everquest game quite quickly. It did not take long before Shawn started having adverse effects in his real-life from playing the virtual Everquest game.

In April of 2000, Shawn got a job at Domino's Pizza in Hudson, WI. Shawn was prompt, dependable, hard-working, and trustworthy. Within the next couple of months, Shawn found a room to rent and moved out of my house. He was becoming a contributing adult in society.

By the end of that summer, Shawn had changed drastically. He quit his job because he played the virtual Everquest game so much that he was having grand-mal seizures. Because he had no job or money, he stopped paying his rent and soon was stealing food from his landlord. Shawn was becoming someone I did not know. He became withdrawn, depressed, and anti-social. Shawn had no contact with anyone other than his landlord, and me, his mother. When I went to see him, Shawn made me fully aware that he did not appreciate my visits. I worried about him. In September 2000, Shawn was evicted because he had not paid his rent since July.

I agreed to let Shawn move back into my house if he would seek professional help. Shawn agreed. I contacted a therapist in Hudson for Shawn to see so he could get some help for his video gaming rowing addiction problem. After several sessions, the therapist informed me, right in front of Shawn, "You should be glad Shawn is not addicted to drugs or alcohol." The therapist did not consider Shawn's excessive video game playing a problem. I thought, how could this not be a problem? My son, Shawn, just lost his job, apartment, health, and car because he was playing the virtual Everquest game constantly, excluding every other part of his life. Since the therapist did not see his gaming as a significant problem, this gave Shawn the green light to continue with his excessive video game playing. Shawn looked directly at me and said, "This is your problem now Mom, not mine." In Shawn's mind, there was nothing wrong with him playing the virtual Everquest game all the time.

Shawn was now solidly addicted to this virtual Everquest game. I could not believe it. I was in Alcoholics Anonymous (AA) for 20 years. I was aware of how addicts behaved. I was prepared to take specific steps if my children ever got addicted to drugs or alcohol. Never did I think my child would get addicted to a video game! Unfortunately, there was nowhere to go for help! This craziness and ongoing drama lasted for several months.

Shawn took his own life 11/20/2001

I knew Shawn needed more help than I could give him. In December of 2000, I was led to contact a long-term support program in our county. They help people who have long-term challenges to be independent.

Diagnosis.

Shawn qualified for this program thorough a series of mental tests. The human brain is fragile. After one year of playing, the virtual Everquest game was a major factor in the negative changes in Shawn's life and character. Before Everquest, Shawn was a kind, creative, friendly, funny, hard-working, and sensitive young man. One year later, after his twenty-first birthday, Shawn was diagnosed as a dull, humorless, lonely, depressed person. It seemed like Shawn was a shell of the human being he used to be.

Treatment.

Shawn was allowed to join the program called Long Term Support. He went into a group home. I thought living in the group home worked well for Shawn. There was no computer there, and he had "some" socialization. The staff took Shawn to his doctor, psychiatrist, and therapist appointments. They made sure he was taking his medications.

Eventually, I met with Shawn's psychiatrist, Dr. Ei. I asked him for his solution to get Shawn off the Everquest game. Dr. Ei said that he had talked with Shawn about his excessive gaming. Shawn said that was the only thing he liked to do. Dr. Ei agreed with Shawn that he could keep playing the Everquest game. To me, this was utterly ridiculous. It was like telling an alcoholic that if drinking is the only thing you like to do, keep drinking! Or telling a drug addict that if heroin is all you like to do, keep doing it. I was disappointed that Dr. Ei did not recognize Shawn's excessive gaming as a problematic behavior, that was becoming an addiction. For my son, the results were the same as any other addict – either you get clean (get off your drug of choice), get locked up (go insane or go to prison), or you die.

Shawn was doing so well at the group home that in May of 2001, he got a job at Papa Murphy's Pizza in Hudson, WI. By June, with the support of his long-term support program, Shawn moved into his apartment against the wishes of his stepfather and me. We felt Shawn needed the supervision and help he was getting in the group home. Our opinion was disregarded.

Shawn often came to my house to play the virtual Everquest game when I was not there. He did not talk to his real-life friends or us much anymore. He quit going on outings with his little brother, Tony. Shawn said his "real" friends were in the game now. He only trusted them. This thought saddened me greatly. I tried to explain to Shawn that the characters in the video games were only pixels and not real people. He did not believe me, and he did not care. His loss of touch with reality was frightening.

Shawn was having grand mal seizures again because of his excessive gaming. These seizures were so upsetting to us that Shawn was banned from playing the Everquest game in our home. Shawn got very angry with us for doing this. He did not care about himself or us, his family. All Shawn cared about was playing the game. That became his all-consuming addiction.

In August 2001, Shawn got a second-hand computer at his apartment. He said he wanted it to get Microsoft certified to get a better job. Shawn ought to have been happy now. He had a good job, a place of his own, and his own computer. Soon after this, Shawn stopped all communication with us. He disconnected his phone and would not answer his door when we came to visit. I had to go to or call his work to see or talk to him.

On Halloween night, October 31, Shawn agreed to come over to the house for a visit. I had not seen him since August, except at his work. While he was at my home, Shawn told me that he had stopped taking his medications. I was shocked and dumbfounded. "Why???" I asked him. He answered, "Because."

The Final Battle

The final battle to get my son back started the week before Thanksgiving. The next day, I contacted his caseworker to find out what was going on. She said she had not been to Shawn's place since August. That was when he got that computer! He had not been going to his doctor appointments since August. She said they had not been able to tell me about this information before because I was not Shawn's legal guardian. I was very concerned. Shawn's caseworker did say that she had set up an appointment with Shawn right after Thanksgiving. Unfortunately, that appointment never took place.

Our family was invited to my sister Maureen's place for the Thanksgiving meal. On Thanksgiving Day morning, I went to pick up Shawn at his apartment so that we could ride together. He did not answer his door. I broke into his apartment and saw my son, Shawn, in his bedroom, sitting on his rocking chair in front of his computer. There was a .22 rifle propped up by his side. Shawn had shot himself and was dead. Shawn's computer was still on, and that virtual Everquest game was on the computer screen. I ran out of his apartment and collapsed in the hallway.

So much had happened in the last year and a half that destroyed our mother-son relationship. Shawn became so influenced by the game that he did not need his family anymore. He started having seizures again. Shawn got his apartment and bought his computer. Shawn stopped having contact with his family. Shawn stopped going to his doctor's appointments and quit taking his medications. Unbeknownst to me, something so tragic happened in Shawn's on-line world that he quit gaming on October 30, 2021. His real-life was empty. He had left it for the game. Shawn didn't know how to come back to his real life. There was no support to help him and show him how to do that. The withdrawal from the game became so bad for Shawn that he bought a gun. Then he quit his job.

All of this contributed to Shawn taking his own valuable yet fragile life on November 20, 2001. I often ask myself, "How much did this virtual Everquest game manipulate Shawn to make those choices in his life?" That game seemed to be rapidly sucking Shawn into its fantasy world and isolate him from his real life. It had changed my kind, funny, gentle, loving, hard-working son into a disabled, anti-social, empty shell of a human being. I became furious! My motherly instinct immediately knew that Shawn's death had SOMETHING to do with that video game. Otherwise, why would he shoot himself, sitting in front of the computer with that Everquest game on it? Shawn planned to die that way for a reason. That was the only "suicide note" he left. I know Shawn was sending me a message, so his death would not be in vain. "Mom, by playing this video game, I lost my reason to live. I no longer have a real life. I chose to die like this so you can warn others." And I lost the battle to get my son, Shawn, out of the grip of that virtual Everquest video game.

Books available on Amazon.

For the rest of the story of Shawn's life, read the book "Your Son Did NOT Die in Vain" by Liz Woolley with John M. Langel, Sr. It is available in three forms 1) color, 2) black & white and as a 3) eBook. To learn more about Video Game addiction get "The Toxic Dangers of Video Games." These books can be purchased from Amazon.com.

A true story about the devastating effects of video gaming addiction.
Written by Liz Woolley with John M. Langel, Sr.

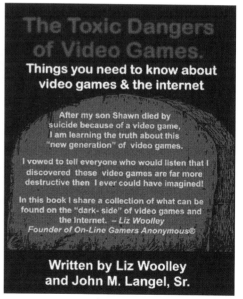

The Toxic Dangers of Video Games.
Things you need to know about video games & the internet

After my son Shawn died by suicide because of a video game, I am learning the truth about this "new generation" of video games.

I vowed to tell everyone who would listen that I discovered these video games are far more destructive then I ever could have imagined!

In this book I share a collection of what can be found on the "dark-side" of video games and the Internet. – Liz Woolley
Founder of On-Line Gamers Anonymous®

Written by Liz Woolley and John M. Langel, Sr.

Chapter 6. Suicide

Suicide in the US.

This chapter highlights important facts about suicide in the US. This table shows the ten leading causes of death in the US and deaths attributed to each cause.

Rank	10-14	15-24	25-34	35-44	45-54	55-64	All Ages
					Leading Cause of Death in the United States for Select Age Groups (2019)		
					Data Courtesy of CDC		
1	Unintentional Injury 778	Unintentional Injury 11,755	Unintentional Injury 24,516	Unintentional Injury 24,070	Malignant Neoplasms 35,587	Malignant Neoplasms 111,765	Heart Disease 659,041
2	Suicide 534	Suicide 5,954	Suicide 8,059	Malignant Neoplasms 10,695	Heart Disease 31,138	Heart Disease 80,837	Malignant Neoplasms 599,601
3	Malignant Neoplasms 404	Homicide 4,774	Homicide 5,341	Heart Disease 10,499	Unintentional Injury 23,359	Unintentional Injury 24,892	Unintentional Injury 173,040
4	Homicide 191	Malignant Neoplasms 1,388	Malignant Neoplasms 3,577	Suicide 7,525	Liver Disease 8,098	CLRD 18,743	CLRD 156,979
5	Congenital Anomalies 189	Heart Disease 872	Heart Disease 3,495	Homicide 3,446	Suicide 8,012	Diabetes Mellitus 15,508	Cerebro-vascular 150,005
6	Heart Disease 87	Congenital Anomalies 390	Liver Disease 1,112	Liver Disease 3,417	Diabetes Mellitus 6,348	Liver Disease 14,385	Alzheimer's Disease 121,499
7	CLRD 81	Diabetes Mellitus 248	Diabetes Mellitus 887	Diabetes Mellitus 2,228	Cerebro-vascular 5,153	Cerebro-vascular 12,931	Diabetes Mellitus 87,647
8	Influenza & Pneumonia 71	Influenza & Pneumonia 175	Cerebro-vascular 585	Cerebro-vascular 1,741	CLRD 3,592	Suicide 8,238	Nephritis 51,565
9	Cerebro-vascular 48	CLRD 168	Complicated Pregnancy 532	Influenza & Pneumonia 951	Nephritis 2,269	Nephritis 5,857	Influenza & Pneumonia 49,783
10	Benign Neoplasms 35	Cerebro-vascular 158	HIV 486	Septicemia 812	Septicemia 2,176	Septicemia 5,672	Suicide 47,511

Suicide is the second highest cause of death after accidents for 10- to 34-year-olds, fourth for 35-44, fifth for 45-54 and eighth for 55-64.

Data are shown for all ages and select age groups where suicide was one of the leading ten causes of death in 2019. The data are based on death certificate information compiled by the CDC.

https://www.nimh.nih.gov/health/statistics/suicide

From the National Institute of Mental Health: Suicide is now a Leading Cause of Death in the United States According to the Centers for Disease Control and Prevention (CDC) WISQARS Leading Causes of Death Reports, in 2019:

Suicide was the tenth leading cause of death overall in the United States, claiming the lives of over 47,500 people.

o Suicide was the second leading cause of death among individuals between the ages of 10 and 34, and the fourth leading cause of death among individuals between the ages of 35 and 44.

o There were nearly two and a half times as many suicides (47,511) in the United States as there were homicides (19,141).

o Veterans have an adjusted suicide rate that is 52.3% greater than the non-veteran US adult population.

o People who have previously served in the military account for about 13.7% of suicides among adults in the United States.

o In 2019, 1.6% of active service people did a suicide attempt during the previous 12 months.

o Former active-duty service members aged 18-25 years reported making a suicide attempt increased yearly since 2009.

o Data are limited on the rate of suicide among people who identify as sexual minorities. However, research has shown that people who identify as sexual minorities have higher rates of suicide attempts compared to heterosexual people.

o Almost a quarter (23.4%) of high school students identifying as lesbian, gay, or bisexual reported attempting suicide in the prior 12 months.

Factors Contributing to Suicide.

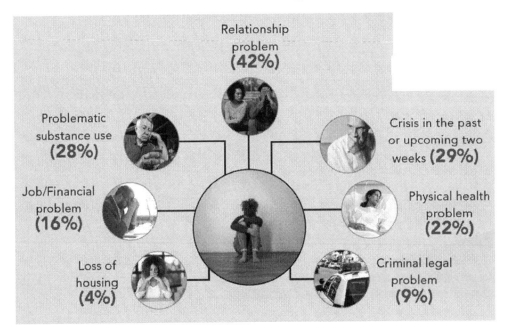

Note: Persons who died by suicide may have had multiple circumstances. Data on mental health conditions and other factors are from coroner/medical examiner and law enforcement reports. It is possible that mental health conditions or other circumstances could have been present and not diagnosed, known, or reported.

SOURCE: CDC's National Violent Death Reporting System, data from 27 states participating in 2015.

Between 1999 and 2019 the suicide death rate increased 33%. In 2020 there were nearly 46,000 making it the 12th leading cause of death in the US. In 2020 it is estimate 12.2 million adults seriously thought about suicide, 3.2 million planned and 1.2 million made a serious attempt.

Suicide Prevention by CDC

Suicide is death caused by injuring oneself with the intent to die. A suicide attempt is when someone harms themselves with any intent to end their life, but they do not die because of their actions.[1]

Many factors can increase the risk for suicide or protect against it. Suicide is connected to other forms of injury and violence. For example, people who have experienced violence, including child abuse, bullying, or sexual violence have a higher suicide risk. Being connected to family and community support and having easy access to health care can decrease suicidal thoughts and behaviors.[2]

Suicide rates increased 30% between 2000–2018 and declined in 2019 and 2020. Suicide is a leading cause of death in the United States,[3] with 45,979 deaths in 2020. This is about one death every 11 minutes.[3] The number of people who think about or attempt suicide is even higher. In 2020, an estimated 12.2 million American adults seriously thought about suicide, 3.2 million planned a suicide attempt, and 1.2 million attempted suicide.

Suicide affects all ages. In 2020, suicide was among the top 9 leading causes of death for people ages 10-64. Suicide was the second leading cause of death for people ages 10-14 and 25-34.[3]

Some groups have higher suicide rates than others. Suicide rates vary by race/ethnicity, age, and other factors, such as where someone lives. By race/ethnicity, the groups with the highest rates were non-Hispanic American Indian/Alaska Native and non-Hispanic White populations. [3] Other Americans with higher-than-average rates of suicide are veterans, people who live in rural areas, and workers in certain industries and occupations like mining and construction. Young people who identify as lesbian, gay, or bisexual have higher rates of suicidal thoughts and behavior compared to their peers who identify as heterosexual.

Suicide and suicide attempts cause serious emotional, physical, and economic impacts. People who attempt suicide and survive may experience serious injuries that can have long-term effects on their health. They may also experience depression and other mental health concerns. The good news is that more than 90% of people who attempt suicide and survive never go on to die by suicide.

Suicide and suicide attempts affect the health and well-being of friends, loved ones, co-workers, and the community. When people die by suicide, their surviving family and friends may experience shock, anger, guilt, symptoms of depression or anxiety, and may even experience thoughts of suicide themselves.

The financial toll of suicide on society is also costly. In 2019, suicide and nonfatal self-harm cost the nation nearly $490 billion in medical costs, work loss costs, value of statistical life, and quality of life costs.

Suicide is preventable and everyone has a role to play to save lives and create healthy and strong individuals, families, and communities. Suicide prevention requires a comprehensive public health approach. CDC developed Preventing Suicide: A Technical Package of Policy, Programs, and Practices pdf icon[PDF – 394 KB] (also available in Spanish pdf icon[PDF – 34 MB]), which provides information on the best available evidence for suicide prevention. States and communities can use the technical package to help make decisions about suicide prevention activities. Strategies range from those designed to support people at increased risk to a focus on the whole population, regardless of risk.

Strengthen economic supports

- Strengthen household financial security
- Housing stabilization policies

Strengthen access and delivery of suicide care

- Coverage of mental health conditions in health insurance policies
- Reduce provider shortages in underserved areas
- Safer suicide care through systems changes

Create protective environments

- Reduce access to lethal means among persons at risk
- Organizational policies and culture
- Community-based policies to reduce excessive alcohol use

Promote connectedness

- Peer norm programs
- Community engagement activities

Teach coping and problem-solving skills

- Social-emotional learning programs
- Parenting skill and family relationship programs

Identify and support people at risk

- Gatekeeper training
- Crisis intervention
- Treatment for people at risk of suicide
- Treatment to prevent re-attempts

Lessen harms and prevent future risk

- Postvention
- Safe reporting and messaging about suicide

The Stigma of Suicide.

In recent years the stigma of suicide has been lessening. Sadly, it is becoming an acceptable solution to life's problems, and more people are doing it. The paragraphs below are sourced from NIH, National Library of Medicine, National Center for Biotechnology Information, in an article titled: The Stigma of Suicide Survivorship and Related Consequences—A Review. "Courtesy of the U.S. National Library of Medicine" https://www.ncbi.nlm.nih.gov/pmc/articles/PMC5033475/

"A suicide survivor is defined here as "someone who has lost a significant other to suicide." For every suicide, there are approximately 18 individuals experiencing major life disruptions during suicide survivorship. Given an annual rate of 800,000 suicides worldwide, up to 14.4 million people might be intimately affected by suicide bereavement every year.

Stigmatization of suicide survivors can be traced back to early historic periods when family members of suicide were faced with being denied a proper burial of the deceased, property confiscation, and excommunication from the community. Although such cultural practices have ceased to exist, there is evidence that negative attitudes towards those bereaved by suicide prevail and that stigmatization has taken more subtle forms of isolation and shunning. Additionally, the ongoing stigmatization of suicide and associated mental illnesses provides further indication that stigma is a persistent part of the grief experiences of suicide survivors.

In recent years, scientists have come to understand stigma as a social process that involves labeling, stereotyping, and rejecting human differences to exert social control. Theoretical conceptualizations further distinguish between two interrelated dimensions across which stigma can be assessed: public stigma and self-stigma. Public stigma refers to "the phenomenon of large social groups endorsing negative stereotypes about and acting against a stigmatized group." Self-stigma describes a process whereby stigmatized individuals perceive social devaluation (perceived stigma), experience actual enactments of stigma in the form of discrimination (enacted stigma), or internalize negative attitudes of others, resulting in an adverse self-image characterized by shame, guilt, maladaptive behaviors, and/or stereotype endorsement (internalized stigma).

This conceptualization illustrates how stigma might interfere with the grieving process of suicide survivors. Negative attitudes within the public can be conveyed to the survivors through various pathways, such as attribution of blame by the survivor's social environment, gossip, or negative media portrayal of the deceased. If suicide survivors internalize these negative attitudes, this could exacerbate existing feelings of shame, self-blame and/or guilt. In order to avoid stigmatization, suicide survivors might also engage in maladaptive behaviors, such as concealment of the cause of death.

Although suicide bereavement appears to largely resemble grieving after other types of loss in terms of symptom severity, there is indication that some suicide survivors are at an increased risk of developing depression, suicide ideation, and a pathological grief reaction, defined as prolonged grief disorder or complicated grief in the bereavement literature. Complications occurring while grieving appear to be related to a range of qualitative themes common in suicide bereavement. Thus, suicide survivors face the burden of finding reasons to explain the death and suffer from feelings of shame about the cause of the death, guilt for not being able to prevent the death, blame directed towards self and others and abandonment and rejection by the deceased. Another factor that characterizes suicide bereavement and that may greatly complicate the grieving process after suicide is the social stigma attached to suicide survivors." **End of NIH article**

Javert's Suicide in Les Miz

One suicide that displays the characteristic behaviors that precede ones taking of their life is the death of Inspector Javert from Victor Hugo's novel Les Misérables because it clearly illustrates the three steps to suicide 1) Situation (desperation), 2) Intolerable Dilemma (Inescapability), 3) The Decision to die. It also contrasts the two covenants, WORK (the law of God) and GRACE (Jesus). Because the story has a strong Christian theme, I have chosen to analyze the interactions between Javert and the main character Jean Valjean as they impact Javert's decision to take his life. The story is set in France in the early 1800s and climaxes in 1832 in the June rebellion in Paris.

Jean Valjean is released from prison after 19 years for stealing a loaf of bread. On parole he meets a priest and becomes a Christian by the priest's demonstration of grace. The priest forgives Jean Val Jean for stealing the churches silver and candlesticks. Jean now a believer breaks parole and in 10 years becomes a successful businessman and Mayor of a French city. The transformation from bitter pagan thief to benevolent Christian is obvious as the plot develops.

Inspector Javert is a police official who pursues Jean Valjean to take him back to prison because of the broken parole. Javert becomes obsessed with catching him. Javert sings the "Stars." Which shows his total commitment to bringing Jean to justice by sending him back to prison. God's law and the fulfillment of justice has become his life's central focus and purpose. Click the link and listen to "Stars."

Javert sings "Stars" from Les Miz

https://www.youtube.com/watch?v=dfoJEYicu7c

There, out in the darkness
A fugitive running
Fallen from God
Fallen from grace
God be my witness
I never shall yield
Till we come face to face
Till we come face to face
He knows his way in the dark
Mine is the way of the Lord
Those who follow the path of the righteous
Shall have their reward
And if they fall, As Lucifer fell
The flames, The sword!
Stars, in your multitudes
Scarce to be counted
Filling the darkness
With order and light
You are the sentinels
Silent and sure

Keeping watch in the night
Keeping watch in the night
You know your place in the sky
You hold your course your aim
And each in your season
Returns and returns
And is always the same
And if you fall as Lucifer fell
You fall in flames!
And so, it must be
For so it is written
On the doorway to paradise
That those who falter and those who fall
Must pay the price!
Lord let me find him
That I may see him
Safe behind bars
I will never rest
Till then, this I swear
This I swear by the stars!

As Jean prepares to flee Javert catches up with him. Jean makes a deal to surrender to go back to prison after three days. In a rapid turn of events Javert is captured by revolutionaries and given to Jean Valjean to be executed as a spy. Watch now!
https://www.youtube.com/watch?v=23wh1h0UWZM

Rather than execute justice by killing Javert, Jean shoots the pistol into the ground and sets him free. Javert the strong advocate of justice has been confronted with grace. Justice has been overcome by grace. That's the GOSPEL but Javert can't tolerate it. He insists that the penalty of the law be enforced even though he has tasted grace.

This next song is in three parts. First, he describes the situation that creates the dilemma grace overcoming the law has put him in. He cannot accept receiving pity or being thankful he has been allowed to live. His whole purpose for living has been taken away. In the second part, he laments grace being superior to justice and will have no part of surrendering justice for grace in Jean giving him back his life. He has entered an intolerable dilemma. And sees no way out. This dilemma has brought him to the third point there is no solution but to die. He makes the decision to take his life. NO place to turn and NO way to go on. He cannot live in a world where grace overcomes the law because God himself has intervened. Listen now.

. Javert's Suicide From Les Miz
https://www.youtube.com/watch?v=IsZdfna1LKA

Who is this man, what sort of devil is he?
To have me caught in a trap and choose to let me go free?
It was his hour at last to put a seal on my fate
Wipe up the past and watch me clean up the slate
All it would take was a flick of his knife
Vengeance was his and he gave me back my life
Damned if I'll live in the debt of a thief
Damned if I'll yield at the end of the chase
I am the law and the law is not mocked.
I'll spit his pity right back in his face.
There is nothing on earth that we share.
It is either Valjean or Javert!

·■■

How can I now allow this man to hold dominion over me?
This desperate man that I have hunted.
He gave me my life. he gave me freedom.
I should have perished by his hand. It was his right
It was my right to die as well, instead I live, but live in hell

110

Can this man be believed? Shall his sins be forgiven?
Shall his crimes be reprieved? And must I now begin to doubt
What I never doubted all those years?
My heart is stone but still it trembles, the world I have known
is lost in shadow. Is he from heaven or from hell?
And does he know, that granting me my life today?
This man has killed me, even so.

****

I am reaching but I fall. And the stars are black & cold.
As I stare into the void. Of a world that cannot hold.
I'll escape now from that world. From the world of Jean Valjean.
There is no where I can turn. There is no way to go on

****

Commonly the decision to die by suicide comes about when a person has concluded that the dilemma or situation, they face has no hope of resolution or even ever getting better. To illustrate the steps to the suicide decision I've divided the previous song into three parts. First, the situation, second his reaction and third his decision.

The Situation. Javert represents justice through enforcement of the law to its full extent. He will not be satisfied until all the penalties from the enforcement of the law are carried out and Jean is returned to prison. After their confrontation Jean has the opportunity to bring justice to Javert by killing him but instead gives him grace and sets him free. Justice recoils at the giving of grace and not the punishment required by justice. Justice and grace are set as opponents in Javert's mind.

The Intolerable Dilemma. Javert is now in a dilemma from which he sees NO escape. Justice would be fulfilled if Jean were to kill him when he was told to by the revolutionaries but instead Jean releases Javert. He is now free without justice being done. Javert CANNOT accept this. In his world justice MUST be carried out, NO exceptions. Grace has cancelled Justice causing Javert to ask questions how far can grace go? Sins, forgiven? Crimes, reprieved? This shakes him to the core his belief that his purpose in life is to fulfill the law. To complete Justice, Javert must die.

The Decision. There is no other option. Grace cannot be accepted. He makes the decision to take his own life. He cannot live in a world with grace. The last eight lines in this song illustrates the Apostle Paul's extensive argument in Roman's 6 that the law drives us to grace and clearly shows the great desperation at the last moments of a life that will end in suicide.

Roman's 6 *What shall we say then? Are we to continue in sin that grace may abound? By no means! How can we who died to sin still live in it? Do you not know that all of us who have been baptized into Christ Jesus were baptized into his death?4We were buried therefore with him by baptism into death, in order that, just as Christ was raised from the dead by the glory of the Father, we too might walk in newness of life.*

For if we have been united with him in a death like his, we shall certainly be united with him in a resurrection like his. We know that our old self was crucified with him in order that the body of sin might be brought to nothing, so that we would no longer be enslaved to sin. For one who has died has been set free from sin. Now if we have died with Christ, we believe that we will also live with him. We know that Christ, being raised from the dead, will never die again; death no longer has dominion over him. For the death he died he died to sin, once for all, but the life he lives he lives to God. So, you also must consider yourselves dead to sin and alive to God in Christ Jesus.

Let not sin therefore reign in your mortal body, to make you obey its passions. Do not present your members to sin as instruments for unrighteousness but present yourselves to God as those who have been brought from death to life, and your members to God as instruments for righteousness. For sin will have no dominion over you since you are not under law but under grace.

What then? Are we to sin because we are not under law but under grace? By no means! Do you not know that if you present yourselves to anyone as obedient slaves, you are slaves of the one whom you obey, either of sin, which leads to death, or of obedience, which leads to righteousness? But thanks be to God, that you who were once slaves of sin have become obedient from the heart to the standard of teaching to which you were committed, and, having been set free from sin, have become slaves of righteousness. I am speaking in human terms, because of your natural limitations. For just as you once presented your members as slaves to impurity and to lawlessness leading to more lawlessness, so now present your members as slaves to righteousness leading to sanctification.

For when you were slaves of sin, you were free in regard to righteousness. But what fruit were you getting at that time from the things of which you are now ashamed? For the end of those things is death. But now that you have been set free from sin and have become slaves of God, the fruit you get leads to sanctification and its end, eternal life. For the wages of sin is death, but the gift of God is eternal life in Christ Jesus our Lord.

Jean Valjean Conversion: When Jean Valjean sings his soliloquy earlier when he became a Christian, his declaration is much like Javerts. But here, for Jean Valjean but it's a decision point to turn to Christ because of grace shown by the bishop:

He told me that I have a soul　　*As I stare into the void*
How does he know　　*To the whirlpool of my sin*
What spirit comes to move my life　　*I'll escape now from that world*
Is there another way to go?　　*From the world of Jean Valjean*
I am reaching, but I fall　　*Jean Valjean is nothing now*
And the night is closing in　　*Another story must begin*

✻✻

Listen here: https://www.youtube.com/watch?v=pJx1pRCey78

At this moment he has died to self to confess the Gospel. In both cases the desperation brought about by the situation has brought them to a decision point. New life for Jean Valjean and death for Javert. Look at the parallel verses

<u>Inspector Javert</u>	<u>Jean Valjean</u>
As I stare into the void.	*As I stare into the void*
Of a world that cannot hold.	*To the whirlpool of my sin*
I'll escape now from that world.	*I'll escape now from that world*
From the world of Jean Valjean.	*From the world of Jean Valjean*
There is no where I can turn.	*Jean Valjean is nothing now*
There is no way to go on	*Another story must begin*

✻✻

Let me summarize with this: The Law can only bring death to men because of our sinful nature we cannot obey it completely. Salvation comes through grace because the law was fulfilled in Christ for us. BY faith we receive the satisfaction of the law in Jesus.

We DIE by the JUSTICE of the LAW, - Javert's suicide

We LIVE by the GRACE Of Christ Jesus, - Jean Valjean

1 Corinthians 15:20-22. But in fact, Christ has been raised from the dead, the first fruits of those who have fallen asleep. For as by a man (Adam) came death, by a man (Jesus Christ) has also come the resurrection of the dead. For as in Adam all die, so also in Christ shall all be made alive.

Two men two different destinies.

Inspector Javert: Javert's life is dedicated to enforcing the law of God. He relies on justice to make the world right. He sings:

"Those who follow the path of the righteous, shall have their reward"

"For so it is written on the doorway to paradise, that those who falter and those who fall. Must pay the price!

His commitment is so strong that adding grace subverts justice and so cannot be accepted. He won't accept the grace of his life being spared. So, the only alternative is death. This rejection of grace is the unforgivable sin spoken of in the Bible. Javert is representative of the "old Covenant" of woks. To be reconciled to God by the law a man must keep ALL the law for all his life. No one can survive justice if this is the only way. Although the law promises life it can only bring death because no one can attain its standard. So, Javert must die!

Jean Valjean: Jean Val jean becomes a believer when shown grace by the bishop in his stealing the silver. He recognizes his sin and looks for an escape. Based on the Bishop's grace Jean asks

He told me that I have a soul. How does he know? What spirit comes to move my life? Is there another way to go?

He finds another way to go and is born again. A new story begins as he is now becoming an honest man. When Jean gave Javert his life he's giving him grace but because Javert cannot accept grace he must receive justice which brings Javier to suicide. Once Javert is dead,

Jean Valjean receives freedom from the pursuit of the law and can die in peace. Jean Valjean is representative of the "New Covenant" and by receiving grace comes to know God. This is the Gospel. Grace brings new life in Christ., the law brings only justice and death.

Chapter 7. Suicide in the Bible.

There are seven examples highlighted here of suicide in the Bible. The best known are King Saul, Samson, and Judas.

Abimelech - Judges 9:50-54.

Then Abimelech went to Thebez and encamped against Thebez and captured it. But there was a strong tower within the city, and all the men and women and all the leaders of the city fled to it and shut themselves in, and they went up to the roof of the tower. And Abimelech came to the tower and fought against it and drew near to the door of the tower to burn it with fire. And a certain woman threw an upper millstone on Abimelech's head and crushed his skull. Then he called quickly to the young man his armor-bearer and said to him, "Draw your sword and kill me, lest they say of me, 'A woman killed him.'" And his young man thrust him through, and he died

Samson - Judges 16: 23-31.

Now the lords of the Philistines gathered to offer a great sacrifice to Dagon their god and to rejoice, and they said, "Our god has given Samson our enemy into our hand." And when the people saw him, they praised their god. For they said, "Our god has given our enemy into our hand, the ravager of our country, who has killed many of us." And when their hearts were merry, they said, "Call Samson, that he may entertain us." So, they called Samson out of the prison, and he entertained them. They made him stand between the pillars. And Samson said to the young man who held him by the hand, "Let me feel the pillars on which the house rests, that I may lean against them." Now the house was full of men and women. All the lords of the Philistines were there, and on the roof, there were about 3,000 men and women, who looked on while Samson entertained. Then Samson called to the LORD and said, "O Lord GOD, please remember me and please strengthen me only this once, O God, that I may be avenged on the Philistines for my two eyes." And Samson grasped the two middle pillars on which the house rested, and he leaned his weight against them, his right hand on the one and his left hand on the other. And Samson said, "Let me die with the Philistines." Then he bowed with all his strength, and the house fell upon the lords and upon all the people who were in it. So, the dead whom he killed at his death were more than those whom he had killed during his life. Then his brothers and all his family came down and took him and brought him up and buried him between Zorah and Eshtaol in the tomb of Manoah his father. He had judged Israel twenty years.

Saul and his sons - I Samuel 31: 1-7.

Now the Philistines were fighting against Israel, and the men of Israel fled before the Philistines and fell slain on Mount Gilboa. And the Philistines overtook Saul and his sons, and the Philistines struck down Jonathan and Abinadab and Malchi-shua, the sons of Saul. The battle pressed hard against Saul, and the archers found him, and he was badly wounded by the archers. Then Saul said to his armor-bearer, "Draw your sword, and thrust me through with it, lest these uncircumcised come and thrust me through, and mistreat me." But his armor-bearer would not, for he feared greatly Therefore Saul took his own sword and fell upon it. And when his armor-bearer saw that Saul was dead, he also fell upon his sword and died with him. Thus, Saul died, and his three sons, and his armor-bearer, and all his men, on the same day together. And when the men of Israel who were on the other side of the valley and those beyond the Jordan saw that the men of Israel had fled and that Saul and his sons were dead, they abandoned their cities and fled. And the Philistines came and lived in them.

Ahithophel - 2 Samuel 17:23.

When Ahithophel saw that his counsel was not followed, he saddled his donkey and went off home to his own city. He set his house in order and hanged himself, and he died and was buried in the tomb of his father.

Zimri - I Kings16;18-19.

And when Zimri saw that the city was taken, he went into the citadel of the king's house and burned the king's house over him with fire and died, because of his sins that he committed, doing evil in the sight of the LORD, walking in the way of Jeroboam, and for his sin which he committed, making Israel to sin.

Judas - Matthew 27: 3-10.

Then when Judas, his betrayer, saw that Jesus was condemned, he changed his mind and brought back the thirty pieces of silver to the chief priests and the elders, saying, "I have sinned by betraying innocent blood." They said, "What is that to us? See to it yourself." And throwing down the pieces of silver into the temple, he departed, and he went and hanged himself. But the chief priests, taking the *pieces of silver, said, "It is not lawful to put them into the treasury, since it is blood money." So, they took counsel and bought with them the potter's field as a burial place for strangers. Therefore, that field has been called the Field of Blood to this day. Then was fulfilled what had been spoken by the prophet Jeremiah, saying, "And they took the thirty pieces of silver, the price of him on whom a price had been set by some of the sons of Israel, and they gave them for the potter's field, as the Lord directed me."*

Biblical Analysis

Abimelech: He was killed by subordinate at his request to avoid it being said by others he was "killed by a woman" from a women's millstone attack.

Samson: He was crushed to death by collapsing temple. Samson pulls Dagon's temple down to destroy God's enemies.

Saul and his armor bearer: To avoid being taken captive by the Philistines, both fall on their swords.

Ahithophel: He was disappointed that his counsel to Absalom to conquer King David was not followed, died by hanging

Zimri: Rather than surrender his city he burned the palace down and died in the fire.

Judas: He was the betrayer of Jesus, died by hanging.

We've seen seven examples of suicide yet nowhere in the Bible is it set aside as a particularly heinous sin. Our culture has made it shameful, the Bible does not. As a Bible believer I believe we should do what we can to prevent it. We also should bring our own grief to the survivors. I know now how bad survivors need it.

Jesus said: Blessed are they that mourn: for they shall be comforted. Matthew 5:4

In all four Gospels Jesus refers to death as sleep before he raises one back to life. In the synoptics it's the servant's maid and in John it's Lazarus.

When Jesus entered the house of the synagogue leader, He saw the flute players and the noisy crowd. "Go away," he told them. "The girl is not dead, but asleep." And they laughed at Him. Matthew 9:23-24

He went inside and asked, "Why all this commotion and weeping? The child is not dead, but asleep." Mark 5:39

When He entered the house, He did not allow anyone to go in with Him except Peter, John, James, and the child's father and mother. Meanwhile, everyone was weeping and mourning for her. But Jesus said, "Stop weeping; she is not dead but asleep." And they laughed at Him, knowing that she was dead. Luke 8:51-53

After He had said this, He told them, "Our friend Lazarus has fallen asleep, but I am going there to wake him up." His disciples replied, "Lord, if he is sleeping, he will get better." They thought that Jesus was talking about actual sleep, but He was speaking about the death of Lazarus. So, Jesus told them plainly, "Lazarus is dead, and for your sake I am glad I was not there, so that you may believe. But let us go to him." John 11:11-14

Two conclusions I make from these passages. First, Jesus does not regard death as an end but a transition to a different state. The soul has left the body to go to another place from. which it

121

can return on the command of God. Second, they go to the place of the dead illustrated in Luke's story,

The Rich Man and Lazarus

Now there was a rich man dressed in purple and fine linen, who lived each day in joyous splendor. And a beggar named Lazarus lay at his gate, covered with sores and longing to be fed with the crumbs that fell from the rich man's table. Even the dogs came and licked his sores.

One day the beggar died and was carried by the angels to Abraham's side. And the rich man also died and was buried. In Hades, where he was in torment, he looked up and saw Abraham from afar, with Lazarus by his side.

So, he cried out, 'Father Abraham, have mercy on me and send Lazarus to dip the tip of his finger in water and cool my tongue. But Abraham answered, 'Child, remember that during your lifetime you received your good things, while Lazarus received bad things. But now he is comforted here, while you are in agony. And besides all this, a great chasm has been fixed between us and you, so that even those who wish cannot cross from here to you, nor can anyone cross from there to us.'

'Then I beg you, father,' he said, 'send Lazarus to my father's house, for I have five brothers. Let him warn them, so that they will not also end up in this place of torment.'

But Abraham replied, 'They have Moses and the prophets; let your brothers listen to them.'

'No, father Abraham,' he said, 'but if someone is sent to them from the dead, they will repent.'

Then Abraham said to him, 'If they do not listen to Moses and the prophets, they will not be persuaded even if someone rises from the dead.' John 16:19-31

These passages are a description of real events NOT a parable because when Jesus tells a parable he NEVER uses a person's name. He would be lying to us if he used a name, and it was not a real person. This story teaches that here is a place, Sheol in the Hebrew, where the dead stay as disembodied souls in two separate groups. One in a state of bliss (Abraham's Bosom) and one in a state of torment where the rich man was waiting. Both groups awaiting final judgement to receive their eternal destiny, HEAVEN, or HELL.

In the Apostles Creed when it refers, to "he descended into hell," Jesus' going to Sheol to take the elect from Abraham's Bosom to be in heaven with the Father. He leaves the other group there, in torments, until they will appear at the final judgement which is described as appearing before the "Great White Throne".

"Then I saw a great white throne and the One seated on it. Earth and heaven fled from His presence, and no place was found for them. And I saw the dead, great and small, standing before the throne.

And there were open books, and one of them was the Book of Life. And the dead were judged according to their deeds, as recorded in the books. The sea gave up its dead, and Death and Hades gave up their dead, and each one was judged according to his deeds.

Then Death and Hades were thrown into the lake of fire. This is the second death—the lake of fire. And if anyone was found whose name was not written in the Book of Life, he was thrown into the lake of fire. Revelation 20:11-15

Until Jesus death no sinner could come before God's throne because His justice would destroy them. When he appears to Moses, he only shows his back.

Moses said, "Please show me your glory." And (God) said, "I will make all my goodness pass before you and will proclaim before you my name 'The LORD.' And I will be gracious to whom I will be gracious and will show mercy on whom I will show mercy. But" (God) said, "you cannot see my face, for man shall not see me and live." And the LORD said, "Behold, there is a place by me where you shall stand on the rock, and while my glory passes by, I will put you in a cleft of the rock, and I will cover you with my hand until I have passed by. Then I will take away my hand, and you shall see my back, but my face shall not be seen." Exodus 33:17-23

But the elect have now been declared NOT GUILTY because their death for their sin has been accomplished for them by Jesus. We call this the substitutionary atonement. As saved souls we can stand before the throne and not be destroyed by His justice. In summary, today the dead in Christ wait with Jesus in Heaven as disembodied souls to return with Him. All the other dead wait in the place of the dead for the judgment.

Suicide is NOT The Unforgivable Sin.

Suicide is sin because it breaks the 6th commandment: "Thou shalt not murder." Suicide is self-murder. It is unique because it is the only sin that cannot be repented of after it is done. It is NOT unforgivable because Christ's sacrifice is sufficient to pay for the sins of the redeemed, past, present, and future. Therefore, a true believer that dies by suicide does NOT lose their salvation. There is only one unforgivable sin defined in Scripture: "Blasphemy against the Holy Spirit."

Mathew 12:31-32. The Unpardonable Sin. *"Therefore, I tell you, every sin and blasphemy will be forgiven men, but the* **blasphemy against the Spirit** *will not be forgiven. Whoever speaks a word against the Son of Man will be forgiven, but* **whoever speaks against the Holy Spirit will not be forgiven**, *either in this age or in the one to come."*

Mark 3:28–30. *"Truly I tell you, the sons of men will be forgiven all sins and blasphemies, as many as they utter. But whoever* **blasphemes against the Holy Spirit will never be forgiven; he is guilty of eternal sin."** *Jesus made this statement because they were saying, "He has an unclean spirit."*

Luke 12:10. And everyone who speaks a word against the Son of Man will be forgiven, **but whoever blasphemes against the Holy Spirit will not be forgiven**

Hebrews 6:4-6. It is impossible for those who have once been enlightened, who have tasted the heavenly gift, who have shared in the Holy Spirit, who have tasted the goodness of the word of God and the powers of the coming age — and then have fallen away — to be restored to repentance, because they themselves are crucifying the Son of God all over again and subjecting Him to open shame.

Hebrews 10:26-31. If we deliberately go on sinning after we have received the knowledge of the truth, no further sacrifice for sins remains, but only a fearful expectation of judgment and of raging fire that will consume all adversaries. Anyone who rejected the law of Moses died without mercy on the testimony of two or three witnesses. **How much more severely do you think one deserves to be punished who has trampled on the Son of God, profaned the blood of the covenant that sanctified him, and insulted the Spirit of grace?**

For we know Him who said, "Vengeance is Mine; I will repay," and again, "The Lord will judge His people." It is a fearful thing to fall into the hands of the living God.

1 John 5:16. Whoever believes in the Son of God has this testimony within him; whoever does not believe God has made Him out to be a liar, because he has not believed in the testimony that God has given about His Son.

In all these passages this unforgivable sin is rejection of God and his Gospel by the Spirits call. For example, the "hardening of Pharaoh's heart'" when Israel was in Egypt is an unforgivable sin for Pharaoh. Because the Holy Spirit is sent to call men when he is blasphemed or rejected that person will receive the judgement of GOD. Simply stated it is the rejection of the Gospel to the end of a person's life. It is the fulfillment of Job's wife's advice, "curse God and die!" Study this further in Romans Chapter 3

Chapter 8. Grieving Death BY Suicide.

We have already seen the added grief by death occurring suddenly when NOT expected. Here is a list of potential causes of suicide. Note it encompasses all areas of human interaction.

Death of a loved one.

Divorce.

Separation.

Broken Relationship.

Losing child custody

Unfair child custody.

Loss: job, house, or money.

A serious illness.

A terminal illness.

A serious accident.

Chronic physical pain.

Intense emotional pain.

Loss of hope.

Being victimized.

Loved one victimized.

Physical abuse.

Verbal abuse.

Sexual abuse.

Past unresolved abuse.

Feeling "trapped" in a negative situation.

Feeling that things will never "get better."

Feeling helpless.

Serious legal problems

Criminal prosecution

Incarceration.

Feel "taken advantage of."

Perceived "humiliation."

Perceived "failure."

Alcohol abuse.

Drug abuse.

Not being accepted by family, friends, or society.

Big disappointment.

High expectations then failure.

Bullying.

Low self-esteem

Now we consider two additional factors adding to our grief because the form of death was suicide. They are:

"Why?" the Sixth "W" question.

"What if" statements.

"WHY?" the Sixth "W" Question.

In our previous discussion of the six "W" questions we noted that in anticipated deaths, or sudden and unanticipated deaths, the "Why" question is not answered or even considered. In cases of death by suicide it becomes the most important question. We consider this act so unbelievable that we MUST know the motivations behind this act of desperation. The "Why" question may be somewhat answered if there is a suicide note, but it is rare to know for certain the person's real motives. I made myself a rule to deal with this.

Weep because you <u>don't and won't know</u> why they took their life NOT because you <u>can't find out</u>.

To go on from our grief we must understand that we will not know for certain "Why did he/she kill him/herself?" Stop asking this question. It is UNANSWERABLE. I've met some people who have extended their grief by continuing to try to determine WHY their loved one took their life. You can't know for certain so give it up to Jesus. He is willing to bear all your burdens! As a Christian, I've given that question to Jesus and He can tell me when I see Him.

My faith overcomes my curiosity and rids me of a potential emotional, depressing OBSESSION.

"What If" – Prevention.

This last additional extender of grief is the concept that changed circumstances may have prevented the person's death. It relates to the behavior of the victim, the one grieving or anyone else involved in their lives. This question is a TRAP. You know you can't change the past, yet you assume that it can be changed by your question. That's a foolish assumption that brings nothing to your grief. Here's examples of some "What ifs" that I've heard.

What if they didn't go to the... (site of death)
What if the gun wasn't there?
What if (a broken relationship) didn't happen
What if (divorce) didn't happen
What if (a loved one's death) didn't happen

Now, that I've said don't use the "What If" I'm going to back up just a little bit. In the very early stages of grief, it MAY be helpful to use it in bringing out some of your emotional relief. If you do use it at all, stop soon, no more than 1-2 months, after the death.

One warning, be aware some people will react negatively to the fact that death was by suicide. Terry and I both went to one of my daughter's friend's funeral. I got in line to sign the guest book. Terry went to talk to some of the students she knew like Darren and Paul. The line was long, so I waited. After at least 10 minutes the man behind me tapped my on the shoulder. I turned around.

He said, "I've been a friend of this family for years but haven't been in touch for years because I moved to California years ago. I was here on business and saw the obituary, so I thought I'd pay my respects. I was gone before Buddy's son took over. How old was (Pause)"

I saw he was stuck so I said, "Kenny."

"How old was Kenny."

"44" I answered.

"How did he die?

I hesitated and said one word., "Suicide."

He was obviously shocked. He repeated, "Suicide."

I said, "Yes."

"Are you sure?"

I said, "Yes." again.

He said, "Thank you." Then he stepped out of the line and headed toward the parking lot. As he walked away, he muttered something that I couldn't hear.

I've never told this story to anyone before, except my wife, but now for the first time it makes sense. It appears some people still believe that those that die by suicide are not worthy of sympathy.

As Christians we should mourn ALL deaths, because of deaths origin. That person has gone to final judgement and is bound unchangeably for HEAVEN or HELL. If they were a believer we can rejoice, but if they were not, we can go on to the next part of this book: grieving by Christians for the death of <u>one who never made a profession of faith in Christ.</u> Where are they now? HEAVEN or HELL?

Part 3. Death WITHOUT Faith.
Chapter 9. World Religions

The goal of this chapter is to describe world religions and then contrast atheism /agnosticism with Charlie and Terry's Christianity to prepare for discussion of the third grief - the eternal destiny of unbelieving people: HEAVEN or HELL?

Remember in our study of the origin of death ONLY the Biblical view has it as a temporary intruder. Death is permanent and part of the structure of the Universe in all world religions not based on Scripture. The Bible teaches clearly that there was no death at the beginning (Genesis 1-2) and will be none at the end (Revelation 21-22).

Three Views of God.

With the variety of the worldviews and religions there are only three views of Mankind's position in the world and his possible redemption: 1) God's not relevant, 2) non-Christian religions, where redemption is either not possible or is attained by some human effort, and 3) Christianity. All three answer the same essential question: "What happens to us when we die?"

1) God's Not Relevant. Atheism, Agnosticism, humanism, and materialism take the position that God may or may not exist but, if he does, he is not relevant to human behavior. Humanity will evolve to a better state without aid from a deity. Evolution from microbes to man is the foundation of this view. Their answer to "What happens when we die?" is, we are extinguished and no longer exist. There is no afterlife. Atheists, Agnostics, and Humanists that understand this fully may take their lives as they age because of the hopelessness of this view. Ernest Hemingway and his family are examples of the hopeless nature of this worldview. They ask, "What's the point of suffering the painful aging process?" It is crucial that, as Christians, that we see the hopelessness of this view because we have the "good news" of the Gospel. The "God's not relevant" view is bad news only! There is no good news there, only extinction and nothingness! There is no purpose or meaning to life.

2) Non-Christian Religions. In all other religions, reconciliation with God is either not necessary or is achieved by some human effort with or without the intervention of a deity. In most religions, it is doing good works or keeping of some ritual practices. Most, except for Christianity, have some redemption or escape from death achievable by some aspect of human effort. They recognize the fundamental flaw (sin) in all people but deal with it by rules, religious practice, recycling, ceremony, etc.

All world religions, including Christianity, agree something is wrong with humanity (the sin problem) and its effects lead to death. No one escapes the Grim Reaper. All these other religions rid their adherents of this curse by some form of religious rules, rituals, practices, etc. Man can rescue himself from death. In some religions, it may require the help of a deity, but human effort of some kind is the key to defeating death. In Hinduism, for example, you go round and round in reincarnation until you achieve Nirvana. In Islam, die a martyr and you get seventy-two virgins in heaven. In Judaism, live as close as you can to observing God's law and you might get into heaven. Christianity holds a very different view from all these others.

3) Christianity. Christianity differs from all other worldviews and religions in a very radical way. All men and women are lost and only God can rescue him. No one can rescue him/herself and all are helpless and hopeless in defeating death. All are condemned by both their nature and their actions. Death came through sin as a direct result of man's rebelling against God's law. Man, created in God's image, was given a threefold life: his physical body, his life or soul (also called "life force"), and his spirit, which connected him directly to God. God placed Adam and Eve in the Garden of Eden and put a tree there to test their love and obedience, the Tree of the Knowledge of Good and Evil. By not eating of the tree, they would demonstrate their love for God as an act of their will. They were given the choice to love by obedience or to not love by disobedience. To love or not love is a choice, so they had true free will. They could love God by obeying his command and not eat from the tree. God told them directly that eating from the tree would have the consequence of death. When Adam ate from the tree, he brought the curse of sin and death to all people and all of Creation. His spirit died immediately. His body entered the process of dying, but it would take some time before he physically died. The original curse in Hebrew implies a process of dying not a single moment event. You will begin to die (spiritual death), you will continue to die (aging), and eventually, you will be dead (physical death). All descendants of Adam and Eve are guilty of this rebellion by both birth and practice. We are born sinners and we sin by intent daily. We will all die! NO EXCEPTIONS

When sin entered, the whole creation began to suffer under this bondage. All men and women because they are dead in their spirit cannot and will not seek reconciliation with God. They hate God by nature and practice (Romans Chapters 1–3). The situation is entirely hopeless, and this what makes Christianity unique. God MUST intervene! There is NO other hope! All are destined to HELL and can do nothing to save themselves. If this were the end of the story, Christianity would be the most hopeless religion on earth. But because God intervenes, it's the most hopeful.

Chapter 10. Atheism vs. Christianity. Atheism.

We begin with three Observations about atheism.

o First, atheism's foundations are furthest from Christianity than any other of the world religions. atheism vs Christianity are direct opposites. God does NOT exist vs. God intervenes directly in a person's eternal destiny.

o Second, it denies entirely the supernatural world with the declaration; "There is no God."

o And third, atheists are more likely to become angry when confronted by the claims of Christ than any other group. They find all Jesus' claims very offensive.

Here is another summary of what atheists believe:

o not believing in a god or gods in any form (no deities)

o believing there is no evidence for gods and no reason to believe in the existence of any.

On an atheist Web site when they contrast atheism and Christianity, they cite the murder of several abortion doctors by Christians as a reason Christianity is not true because this breaks the biblical commandment "Do not murder." They neglect to mention the millions of children killed by these same doctors. This plea is reminiscent of the Nazi war criminals' plea in Nuremberg in 1946. They claimed they "broke no law of Germany." This was true because the laws had dehumanized those they murdered. The International Court, which tried the Nazi war criminals, saw through this, and indicted them for crimes against humanity. The charges involved their actions in concentration camps and other death rampages. The court said, "There is a higher law than the ones passed by governments. Morality has absolute standards!" The source, of course, of this judgment is the sixth commandment, which states, "Thou shalt not murder."

This question of moral absolutes is a source of significant contrast between atheism and Christianity. On morality, atheists say: "Atheism does not lead inevitably to any particular moral position ..." In my conversations, I hear them insist on a relative view of morals. For example, what's right in one circumstance is wrong in another. Abortion is desirable in some circumstances and the taking of a human life can be justified if it serves a useful purpose. This relative position on morality is a hallmark of atheism. Then that same atheist declares unequivocally, " There is NO God!" as he makes a claim of omniscience or infinite knowledge. So now we come to the atheist's problem, morals are relative. The fundamental declaration of "no God" is absolute. This relativism and absolute conflict are a contradiction of the highest order. You can't have it both ways! As Mr. Spock would say, "That's illogical!" Or Data, the android in Star Trek, would say, "That doesn't compute!" Atheism is itself a direct contradiction and defies all logic. "There is NO God!" implies the speaker is omniscient. NO man is!!

For example, here's a conversation I had with an atheist.

Charlie: "Are there moral absolutes in the universe like the Ten Commandments?"

Atheist: "Of course not. All moral judgments are dependent on a society's conditions."

Charlie: "Is there a God that created and rules the Universe?"

Atheist: "No! I say that with certainty, absolutely not!"

Charlie: "So when it comes to morality, there are no absolutes, but you make the absolute statement 'There is no God.' You can't have it both ways: absolute and relative. Atheism is a contradiction in the highest order. If you are going to be consistent with your logic, the best an atheist can be is Agnostic! Atheism itself is a logical contradiction!"

Author's Comment. Wow. That always gets a strong reaction, usually with much anger. The logical flaw in their worldview has been found out, and they don't like it. They know there is no way to explain or justify it, so their only recourse is anger to create a smoke screen.

Here are some questions I ask to provoke them to think about their worldview.

➤ If there is no God, then why does it matter to you if anyone believes in Jesus?
➤ Why does my belief in Jesus distress you so much?
➤ Don't I have freedom to believe what I want to?
➤ Why does it make you so angry I believe in God?
➤ If God doesn't exist, why does it matter?
➤ If there is no God, what's your point in saying there is none?

One more challenge: "In the history of the Christian church, many rulers, philosophers, kings, etc. have tried to destroy Christianity. They have even, at times, declared it dead. Why, after many centuries, haven't they succeeded?

In 1776, Voltaire, the French philosopher, announced, "One hundred years from my day there will not be a Bible in the earth except that is looked upon by some antique seeker." One hundred years later, Voltaire was dead, and the Geneva Bible Society was using his house and press to print and store Bibles. One hundred years from the day of Voltaire's prediction, the first edition of his works sold for eleven cents in Paris, but the British government paid the Czar of Russia half a million dollars for an ancient Bible manuscript. —Source: February 15, 2014, 7:00 p.m. Used under fair use guidelines. http://gewatkins.net/my-words-shall-notpass-away

In the flow of history, the greater the persecution of Christian believers, the more rapidly the church has grown. Why is this? The logical explanation is Christianity is true. The more some try to destroy it, the more God preserves it. If Christianity is not true, then there is no point in trying to destroy it. Leave it alone. It should just go out of fashion and disappear. Two thousand years of church history and the continuing impact of Jesus Christ's life, death, and resurrection on individuals are a stark testimony to its truth. Since the early church, thousands have gone to their deaths rather than renounce Christ. Read Foxe's Book of Martyrs for examples. History testifies to Christ's reality! It's really His story.

Agnosticism.

Ask the agnostic this question: "Is there a God?" They will reply, "I don't know if there is a God or not, but if there is, he is not relevant to my life." Most would probably add, "One cannot know for sure if there is or is not a God, but it doesn't matter."

Agnosticism is the position where I sent the atheist when he realized his logical dilemma. Since the atheist doesn't have absolute knowledge, the best he can say is "I don't and can't know." He can't know for certain "there is no God" because he is not omniscient! Both of these two views deny God—the atheist with certainty and the Agnostic with uncertainty.

Here are several Scriptures that address these views from Romans. My Bible titles this section "God's Wrath on Unrighteousness."

For the wrath of God is revealed from heaven against all ungodliness and unrighteousness of men, who by their unrighteousness suppress the truth. For what can be known about God is plain to them because God has shown it to them. For his invisible attributes, namely, his eternal power and divine nature, have been clearly perceived, ever since the creation of the world, in the things that have been made. So, they are without excuse. For although they knew God, they did not honor him as God or give thanks to him, but they became futile in their thinking, and their foolish hearts were darkened. Claiming to be wise, they became fools and exchanged the glory of the immortal God for images resembling mortal man and birds and animals and creeping things.

Therefore, God gave them up in the lusts of their hearts to impurity, to the dishonoring of their bodies among themselves, because they exchanged the truth about God for a lie and worshiped and served the creature rather than the Creator, who is blessed forever! Amen.
—Romans 1:18–25

God calls both atheists and Agnostics fools!

The fool says in his heart, "There is no God." They are corrupt, they do abominable deeds, there is none who does good. The Lord looks down from heaven on the children of man, to see if there are any who understand, who seek after God. They have all turned aside; together they have become corrupt; there is none who does good, not even one. —Psalm 14:1–3

The Bible is clear here. All men know in their hearts there is a God, but they deny it because his presence would make them accountable, and they won't have it. They truly are fools.

Let's define Agnostic more precisely. Agnostics do not deny the existence of God. Instead, they hold that one cannot know for certain whether God exists. Nineteenth-century British scientist Thomas H. Huxley created the term "Agnostic". He believed that only material phenomena were objects of exact knowledge. He made up the word from the prefix a, meaning "without, not," as in amoral, and the noun Gnostic. Gnostic is related to the Greek word gnōsis, "knowledge," which was used by early Christian writers to mean "higher, esoteric knowledge of spiritual things." Hence, Gnostic referred to those with such knowledge. In coining the term agnostic, Huxley was considering "Gnostics" a group of his fellow intellectuals— "ists," as he called them—who had eagerly embraced various doctrines or theories that explained the world to their satisfaction. Because he was a "man without a rag of a label to cover himself with," Huxley coined the term agnostic for himself. Its first published use was in 1870.

Christianity.

Adam created a sin debt (death) that requires all humans to pay for their rebellion against God. That penalty is physical death. We saw earlier all men are already dead in their spirits. Everyone must pay that same debt. No one born by natural process is exempt. There is no human effort that can solve this problem and create a condition where and when men won't die. We are all lost and undone! God alone can offer a solution. The payment of the sin debt is death, and all must die to pay the penalty! That's the bad news.

Now, the good news of the Gospel! God himself came to earth as Jesus, the perfect man, also known as the second Adam. He was not born by the natural process but was miraculously conceived in the virgin's womb. He is not a son of Adam and does not inherit the sin nature. He lived a perfect life obeying all God's law and then sacrificed himself to pay the sin debt owed by all who will believe. Since men will not seek God, God himself has to awaken men to hear the Gospel call to receive the payment of their debt. God's action is first, then man's response! Lazarus in the grave again!

Here's an analogy to help us understand the Gospel. A judge was hearing a case against a young offender in a court of law. The offender, standing before the tribunal, pleads guilty and is sentenced. The judge, then, imposes a severe sentence. After sentencing is pronounced, the offender tells the judge, "I don't have the ability to pay that penalty." Immediately, the judge removes his robe, steps down, approaches the bailiff, and pays the penalty. The judge did this because this offender was his daughter. So, like this judge, God steps in and pays the penalty we can't pay for those he has chosen.

I assume my readers are familiar with the fundamental doctrines of Christianity, so I'm only going to list three summaries. Principles of Christian Fundamentals (1910), the Five Solas and the Apostle's Creed (1st century)

Fundamentals.
US Christian Fundamentalism began at the Niagara Bible Conference in 1910 at the General Assembly of the Presbyterian Church. The conference created "five fundamentals."

1. Full Biblical inspiration and inerrancy of Scripture.
2. The virgin birth of Jesus.
3. Christ's death as the complete atonement for sin.
4. The bodily resurrection of Jesus.
5. And the historical reality of Jesus' miracles.

Five Solas.
1.   **Sola Scriptura,** or "Scripture alone" (literally: "by scripture alone"), asserts that scripture must govern over church traditions and

interpretations which are themselves held to be subject to Scripture. All church traditions, creeds, and teachings must be in unity with the teachings of Scripture as the divinely inspired Word of God.

2.   **Sola Fide**, or "faith alone," asserts that good works are not a means or requisite for salvation. Sola Fide is the teaching that justification (interpreted in Protestant theology as "being declared just by God") is received by faith alone, without any need for good works on the part of the individual.

3.   **Sola gratia**, or "only grace," specifically excludes the countries done by a person as part of achieving salvation. Sola gratia is the teaching that salvation comes by divine grace or "unmerited favor" only, not as something merited by the sinner.

4.   **Solus Christus**, or "only Christ," excludes the priestly class as necessary for sacraments. Solus Christus is the teaching that Christ is the only mediator between God and man, and that there is salvation through no other (hence, the phrase is sometimes rendered in the ablative case, solo Christo, meaning that salvation is "by Christ alone").

5.   **Soli Deo Gloria**, or "glory to God alone," stands in opposition to the veneration or "cult" perceived by many to be present in the Roman Catholic Church of Mary, the mother of Jesus, the saints, or angels. Soli Deo Gloria is the teaching that all glory is to be due to God alone, since salvation is accomplished solely through His will and action — not only the gift of the all-sufficient atonement of Jesus on the cross but also the gift of faith in that atonement, created in the heart of the believer by the Holy Spirit. Adapted from Wikipedia 2/11/17 11:55 am

Apostle's Creed:

- I believe in God, the Father almighty, creator of heaven and earth.
- I believe in Jesus Christ, God's only Son, our Lord, who was conceived by the Holy Spirit, born of the Virgin Mary, suffered

under Pontius Pilate, was crucified, died, and was buried; he descended into hell.

- On the third day, he rose again; he ascended into heaven, he is seated at the right hand of the Father, and he will come to judge the living and the dead.
- I believe in the Holy Spirit, the holy catholic Church, the communion of saints, the forgiveness of sins, the resurrection of the body, and the life everlasting. Amen.

Practical Atheism, Our Family, Our Friends.

Everyone reading this book has family or friends that do not have a relationship with Jesus. We will call them unsaved. All men are born separated from God by their sin and are bound for Hell. In the Greensboro, NC, where I lived, there are hundreds of churches and most of the population attends some form of Christian church on Sunday, yet the Gospel does not significantly impact the culture. Why? A great many church attendees pay their due to God on Sunday and then behave like Atheists, Agnostics, or Materialists the rest of the week. I call this Practical Atheism. Christianity has become a cultural exercise rather than real communion with the living God! Jesus calls believers to a radical transformation (die to yourself, bear your cross, be crucified with Christ), but few show signs of any real-life change. Hence, we have what is called either Marginal Christianity or Practical Atheism It's a common foundation in many liberal and even some conservative Christian churches, not commonly accepted as a separate religion. I feel compelled to explain it because it is so prevalent in the US. There are many people, attending churches, who call themselves Christians that show no fruit of a walk with Jesus. While searching the Web for this book, I found the following article by J. Robert Hanson, which clearly defines this religious situation. It is used by permission of the author.

Marginal Christianity! by J. Robert Hanson

I begin by asking for your patience to continue reading past my first opening sentence. Ready for it, here it is—*Marginal Christianity* is a bane upon this world. There, I wrote it; are you still with me? Let me try to explain. Of almost 40 years of knowing Jesus Christ, I've noticed that believers (and a whole lot of folks outside the faith) understand exactly what marginal Christianity is! And of all those who have this knowledge only one thing is as certain as the sun rising—no two people will agree exactly on the definition of marginal Christianity. I remember in younger years my involvement with a Christian band. We were taught to shy away from playing "Rock" music. The funny thing was, nobody could give me a definitive answer as to what constitutes "Rock Music"—people just knew it when they heard it. How easy it is to label something you don't like. If the music didn't suit the individual's taste, it was Rock music.

Marginal Christianity is very much the same; it's like knowing good art when you see it! The instinctively assertive look at the inherently passive and imply "you're not doing enough; you're a marginal Christian." All the while the passive returns the favor and points to the assertive and declares, "You're way too legalistic." Marginal Christianity generally comes in all shapes and sizes according to an individual's discernment of God's will. Of course, the intensity varies from person to person, but the results are the same—a sad condemnation of loving brethren.

Here's a thought—maybe marginal Christianity has nothing to do with how much or little one does. Could it be that deliverance from a marginal Christian life is as easy as the word *surrender?* What God is looking for are individuals that yield to him wholly: spirit, soul, and body. That at least is what it appears Paul is instructing the Thessalonians when he writes in

1 Thessalonians 5:23 *Now may the God of peace himself sanctify you completely and may your whole spirit and soul and body be kept blameless at the coming of our Lord Jesus Christ.*

Marginal Christianity is nonexistent in the sanctified life. Purity and holiness are visible as the surrendered heart lives in unobstructed service to Jesus—no matter the personality. I've met very godly people whom I would never have known existed but for some demonstration of surrendered service to God. Maybe surrender is setting up for a worship meeting on a Sunday. Perhaps yielding is slicing apples or making lunches for God's people to enjoy. Maybe surrender is just going about everyday life exhibiting a desire to live for Jesus! Surrender is that silent testimony of God's grace striking fear into the heart of marginal Christianity every time it's tried.

Simply put, marginal Christianity is the life that refuses to surrender everything to the One who gave everything. That's the true bane upon the world. Paul again gives us a picture of what this surrender looks like.

Romans 12:1-2 reads: *I appeal to you therefore, brothers, by the mercies of God, to present your bodies as a living sacrifice, holy and acceptable to God, which is your spiritual worship. Do not be conformed to this world, but be transformed by the renewal of your mind, that by testing you may discern what is the will of God, what is good and acceptable and perfect.*

Deliverance from a marginal Christian life is just that simple—total surrender. Folks who live without yielding everything to Jesus know who they are. No one needs to say to them "You're not doing enough" thus labeling as a marginal Christian. It's always a look at the Savior that inspires me to ask, "What more can I do for you, Lord?" and surrender to His will. If you sense a marginal Christianity in your life, the answer is not more doing but total surrender to Him. Let me finish with a quote from Andrew Murray, *"God does not ask you to give the perfect surrender in your strength, or by the power of your will; God is willing to work it in you.*

J. Robert Hanson.

http://jroberthanson.wordpress.com/2011/04/08/marginal-christianity/

Summary

Before I get into grieving unbelief, I want to make some closing comments about the war between atheism and Christianity. I'm going to test the reliability of both the atheist and Christian worldviews. Then, I'll get to recommendations for personal grieving

Atheism is summarized by the declaration, "There is NO GOD!" Since this is an absolute negative statement, it can't be proven to be true or false by logical reasoning. Most scientists will agree, "You cannot prove or disprove a negative hypothesis." The statement "There is NO GOD!" because it is absolute it implies omniscience or TOTAL knowledge of the whole Universe. NO human is omniscient; therefore, atheism cannot NOT be considered a valid worldview because it has no logical or scientific roots. The best atheists should be able to come up with is, "I have faith there is NO God." That is an Agnostic view NOT an atheistic one.

Therefore, there is no such thing as a real Atheist, but only lying Agnostics making demonstrably false claims.

On the other side Christianity has a solid basis in both history and logic. In history, because the historical documentation is superior to all other ancient historical events. In logic, because both fulfilled prophecy and 2000 years of lives changed by the faith are sufficient proof to its truth. When a person investigates the claims of Jesus they often come to faith.

Christianity's' truth has been and is confirmed by both History and Logic for more than 2,000 years.

For example, read "Who Moved the Stone" by Frank Morison. https://www.amazon.com/s?k=who+moved+the+stone&crid=3J9PG UTJH83WB&sprefix=who+moved+the+stone%2Caps%2C88&ref=nb_ sb_noss_1

Since death is an essential part of an Evolution created world, it is impossible for Christians to accept evolution as the source of the origin of mankind. Death is either permanent or temporary, but it can't be both!! Ask yourself, "Why would God use an evil intruder, death, to bring about the origin of humankind?"

Chapter 11. Grieving Death without Faith.

Judgement: One Destiny, Grief, or Joy.

We now get to the third and most serious grief Terry and I experienced, grieving a person that was "without faith." So far, we've grieved for our loved one's sudden unexpected death by their own hand. Now we must deal with their eternal destiny after death. The Bible is clear ALL will be judged when they die.

"And just as it is appointed for man to die once, and after that comes judgment, so Christ, having been offered once to bear the sins of many, will appear a second time, not to deal with sin but to save those who are eagerly waiting for him. Hebrews 9:27-28

As Christians we believe, there are only two possibilities HEAVEN or HELL. ALL men deserve HELL, but God chooses to bestow his grace on some men and women called the "elect.". This decision was made before time began and can't be changed. Their name is written in the "Lambs Book of Life."

"Then I saw a great white throne and him who was seated on it. From his presence earth and sky fled away, and no place was found for them. And I saw the dead, great and small, standing before the throne, and books were opened. Then another book was opened, which is the book of life. And the dead were judged by what was written in the books, according to what they had done. And the sea gave up the dead who were in it, Death and Hades gave up the dead who were in them, and they were judged, each one of them, according to what they had done. Then Death and Hades were thrown into the lake of fire. This is the second death, the lake of fire. And if anyone's name was not found written in the book of life, he was thrown into the lake of fire." Revelation 20:11-15

147

Final Resolution for Our Grief

God alone knows who is elect, so we evangelize all men letting God call those whom he has chosen. For these reasons our grieving STOPS because:

The elect going to Heaven are already determined. Nothing we can do NOW can change that destiny.

This does NOT mean we stop praying for God to save those we love that are still alive. Remember, God often saves the most unlikely. ASSUME all men are elect and give the power of choice over to God. You never had the power to save anyone. To think so would be putting yourself in God's place.

We must now turn this result over to Jesus and rely on his promises. If we don't end our grieving now, then it will become endless. Jesus said:

"Come to me, all who labor and are heavy laden, and I will give you rest. Take my yoke upon you, and learn from me, for I am gentle and lowly in heart, and you will find rest for your souls. For my yoke is easy, and my burden is light." Matthew 11:28-30

"He will wipe away every tear from their eyes, and death shall be no more, neither shall there be mourning, nor crying, nor pain anymore, for the former things have passed away." Revelation 21:4

"For while we were still weak, at the right time Christ died for the ungodly. For one will scarcely die for a righteous person—though perhaps for a good person one would dare even to die—but God shows his love for us in that while we were still sinners, Christ died for us. Since, therefore, we have now been justified by his blood,

much more shall we be saved by him from the wrath of God. For if while we were enemies we were reconciled to God by the death of his Son, much more, now that we are reconciled, shall we be saved by his life. More than that, we also rejoice in God through our Lord Jesus Christ, through whom we have now received reconciliation."
Romans 5:6-11

Now we move to the Gospel which is the foundation for all I've written. Without my faith I don't know how I could get beyond our loved one's death. I challenge every reader, "Can your view of reality carry you through the tragedies of life?" IF NOT, the next chapter will answer that need.

Chapter 12. From Death to Life, The Gospel.

We have finished our writing about levels of grief. In this chapter we will review the basis of our faith in Jesus Christ. If you have read this far, this chapter will answer why we came to the conclusions we published. Our foundation has and will always be Scripture.

Romans 10:9-13 ...if you confess with your mouth that Jesus is Lord and believe in your heart that God raised him from the dead, you will be saved. For with the heart, one believes and is justified, and with the mouth one confesses and is saved. For the Scripture says, "Everyone who believes in him will not be put to shame." For there is no distinction between Jew and Greek; for the same Lord is Lord of all, bestowing his riches on all who call on him. For "everyone who calls on the name of the Lord will be saved."

Acts 16:30-31 ... "Sirs, what must I do to be saved?" And they said, "Believe in the Lord Jesus, and you will be saved, you and your household

Acts 8:37 Then Philip said, "If you believe with all your heart, you may (be baptized)." And he answered and said, "I believe that Jesus Christ is the Son of God."

Men are dead in their sin.

People can't and won't respond to the Gospel by their own will because they are dead in their sin. God, the Holy Spirit, must enliven them first. Men, separated from God by sin, must pay sins penalty, death. ALL men die. There are no exceptions. From the Bible: "For the wages of sin is death" (Romans 8:23) and "the soul that sins., it shall die" (Ezekiel 18:4c). A human can only resolve this dilemma by dying and becoming eternally separated from God in HELL. So, all men are condemned to HELL from birth. If you believe his then:

- "You are separated from God because of your sin."
- "As a sinner, you must pay the penalty of death."
- "You are condemned, after death, to Hell by your sin."
- "You cannot ever do enough, in this life, to pay the sin debt."
- "There is no hope in anything you can do to merit Heaven."
- "You are helpless, hopeless, lost, and undone before a God."

Paying the Sin Debt, God's Solution.
- "Since you can't pay this debt, God must pay it for you. A perfect man must die for payment. That's Jesus."
- "Someone who can pay the debt has to pay it. No son or daughter of Adam can pay it for you because they owe their own debt. Only a perfect man, without sin, can pay someone else's debt. Jesus is the only one that can, and he did."
- "If your debt is going to be paid, either you can pay it, or someone who has the ability to pay can pay it for you.   No other man can pay, because they all have their own debt, and no one can pay twice. Jesus came for that purpose, as a perfect man, to pay sinners' debts."

Invitation.
- Let's summarize. You are lost and have a sin debt you can't pay. Jesus has paid that debt for you by dying on the cross. God has made you alive, but you must now move from death to life. Do you want to receive Christ's payment and enter a new life with Jesus?
- *Just so, I tell you, there will be more joy in heaven over one sinner who repents than over ninety-nine righteous persons who need no repentance. —Luke 15:7*

- *Just so, I tell you, there is joy before the angels of God over one sinner who repents. —Luke 15:10*
- *Therefore, if anyone is in Christ, he is a new creation. The old has passed away; behold, the new has come. 2 Corinthians 5:17*

The Raising of Lazarus.

Jesus' raising of Lazarus, from the Gospel of John, gives us an excellent picture of how God brings men salvation.

READ. John 11:17–44.

Lazarus has been dead four days. His body has begun to decay. It stinks! Being dead, the body physically can't come back to life by any natural process. It requires a miracle to return to life. All people are dead in their sin and unable to hear! Dead men can't hear or be awakened. They are DEAD!

Jesus comes to the grave, thanks the Father for what he is about to do, and then calls Lazarus by name. But his body can't live! How can he respond? His body is rotting and stinking. He's been dead four days! The first thing that must happen is the power of God comes on his dead body to restore it to a condition of life so he can hear Christ's call. All the death and decay must be taken away. The body must be in a condition of life with awareness. This preparation by the Holy Spirit brings life and softens the heart. Ezekiel 11:19 says, "And I will give them one heart, and I will put a new spirit within you, and I will take the stony heart out of their flesh and will give them a heart of flesh."

Jesus spoke of thus many times when he said, "He who has ears to hear, let him hear." God/Jesus grants the ability to hear.

Mathew 13:13-14This is why I speak to them in parables: 'Though seeing, they do not see; though hearing, they do not hear or understand.' In them the prophecy of Isaiah is fulfilled: 'You will be ever hearing but never understanding; you will be ever seeing but never perceiving.

Luke 8:10 (Speaking to his disciples) He replied, "The knowledge of the mysteries of the kingdom of God has been given to you, but to others I speak in parables, so that, 'though seeing, they may not see; though hearing, they may not understand.'

Do YOU have ears to hear?

Lazarus' body is now alive, by the power of the Holy Spirit, and aware of his surroundings. God opens his ears to hear. Jesus said many times "Give them ears to hear." Remember dead men hear nothing. Jesus spoke of being able to hear in the Gospels three times with the parable of the Sower. "He who has ears to hear, let him hear."

Paul spoke of this spiritual deafness of Israel in Romans 11:8. "As it is written, "God gave them a spirit of stupor, eyes that would not see and ears that would not hear, down to this very day." The first action in salvation then is God acting to prepare a person by making him or her alive to hear the Gospel. God alone can do this. Dead men, in their sin, cannot respond to a Gospel call without God acting first by giving them ears to hear. That is why, as a believer, we must always pray for God, the Holy Spirit, to act before we witness to Christ's transforming power. Dead men can't and don't hear us!

Lazarus is now aware laying on the cold stone, alive and able to hear Christ's call. He is still in the cave tomb, so the first thing he does in response is get up and walk out of the grave. That's man's responsibility to respond to the Gospel call.

Will YOU hear: Jesus' call, come out of the grave?

Now he walks out, but the grave clothes, which represent his sin, still significantly encumber him. Although his sin debt is fully paid, his lifestyle, habits, etc. are all still with him. Others must help him shed the grave clothes.

Unwrapping him is a picture of discipleship. An excellent example of how to do this is CBMC's "Operation Timothy." A mature believer called a Paul, teaches a new believer, called Timothy, the basics of Christian living. I was Timothy when I was a new believer in Greenville, South Carolina. Since then, I have been a Paul and seen men grow in Christ as they went through this program.

Will YOU receive discipleship training?

In summary, people are dead and unable to do anything to save themselves from God's righteous judgment. God saves men by first making them alive to hear, and then the person responds to the Gospel that they've heard. Human agency is required to complete this process, but it *must* begin with God giving life to the dead. The new believer is faced with many instructions in God's Word, but the one we'll focus on here is the Great Commission.

"Now the eleven disciples went to Galilee, to the mountain to which Jesus had directed them. And when they saw him, they worshiped him, but some doubted. And Jesus came and said to them, 'All authority in heaven and on earth has been given to me. Go therefore and make disciples of all nations, baptizing them in the name of the Father and of the Son and of the Holy Spirit, teaching them to observe all that I

154

have commanded you. And behold, I am with you always, to the end of the age.'" —Matthew 28:16–20

The Spiritual Equations.

Humankind = All men born from Adam and Eve including everyone that lives on planet Earth, except Jesus Christ. Jesus was not a son of Adam because of the virgin birth. That's why he's called the second Adam.

God's Law = The moral law God gave to Moses and Israel in the Old Testament. It's God's rules for all humankind's behavior, and it must be kept entirely in every detail to satisfy God's justice.

Good Works = Actions men and women do to try to please God.

Grace/Faith = The Gospel of Jesus Christ as given in the New Testament. The payment for sin made by Jesus' death on the cross, confirmed by his resurrection.

Hell = The result of God's justice applied to all humankind. Everyone! No exceptions. No one can be good enough because the standard is perfection, and no son or daughter of Adam can ever be perfect in this life. As is commonly said, "I'm only human!"

Heaven = God's reward to those that have been called, justified, sanctified, and finally glorified. The Bible calls them the elect. They have received grace and lived by faith. Here are the two equations:

Note the common threads in both equations. Both start with humankind and God's law. Both contain good works, but they are on opposite sides of the equation. The results are direct opposites: HELL, or HEAVEN

Humankind
+
God's Law
+
Good Works

=

Sheol, Hell
+
Lake of Fire, with the 2nd DEATH

Humankind
+
God's Law
+
Grace & Faith

=

Good Works
+
HEAVEN with Eternal LIFE

Conclusions we can draw from these equations are:

1) Without grace/faith, no amount of good works can bring us to Heaven!

2) Hell is the only result humankind can expect based on his/her personal merit.

3) With grace and faith, humanity receives Heaven. Good works result in his/her life because of gratitude to God for "so great a salvation."

Conclusion.

You have seen many different aspects of grieving in the three levels I've described. Now I want to summarize all these aspects under the shadow of the Christian worldview. When a loved one dies the immediate reaction is one of sorrow and grief. WHY. If death is part of the operation of the Universe, then why grieve? All men and women will die it's not "if?" it's "when?" BUT you know death should not be part of this world because your internal monitor we call the conscience tells you so. This is well documented in Paul's letter to the Romans in chapters 1:18-25.

For the wrath of God is revealed from heaven against all ungodliness and unrighteousness of men, who by their unrighteousness suppress the truth. For what can be known about God is plain to them because God has shown it to them. For his invisible attributes, namely, his eternal power and divine nature, have been clearly perceived, ever since the creation of the world in the things that have been made. So, they are without excuse. For although they knew God, they did not honor him as God or give thanks to him, but they became futile in their thinking, and their foolish hearts were darkened. Claiming to be wise, they became fools, and exchanged the glory of the immortal God for images resembling mortal man and birds and animals and creeping things. Therefore, God gave them up in the lusts of their hearts to impurity, to the dishonoring of their bodies among themselves, because they exchanged the truth about God for a lie and worshiped and served the creature rather than the Creator, who is blessed forever! Amen.

AS with all knowledge of God men suppress the truth that DEATH is an intruder and NOT intended by God' original creation. This is the first important difference between the Christian view and the world.

DEATH is Transitory NOT Permanent!
Death entered in Genesis chapter 3 NOT chapter 1. The world was perfect and complete in Chapters 1 and 2. The second factor is that death is NOT the end of a person's existence. Death is not final.

DEATH is a Transition NOT an END
Jesus provides a certain hope in many places for life continued after death. At the end in Revelation 20 D death is cast into the lake of fire to be removed from the new creation for everlasting, eternity future.

DEATH is Destroyed, ONLY Life Remains
"Then I saw a great white throne and him who was seated on it. From his presence earth and sky fled away, and no place was found for them. And I saw the dead, great and small, standing before the throne, and books were opened. Then another book was opened, which is the book of life. And the dead were judged by what was written in the books, according to what they had done. And the sea gave up the dead who were in it, Death and Hades gave up the dead who were in them, and they were judged, each one of them,

according to what they had done. Then Death and Hades were thrown into the lake of fire. This is the second death, the lake of fire. And if anyone's name was not found written in the book of life, he was thrown into the lake of fire.

Then I saw a new heaven and a new earth, for the first heaven and the first earth had passed away, and the sea was no more. And I saw the holy city, new Jerusalem, coming down out of heaven from God, prepared as a bride adorned for her husband. And I heard a loud voice from the throne saying, "Behold, the dwelling place of God is with man. He will dwell with them, and they will be his people, and God himself will be with them as their God. He will wipe away every tear from their eyes, and death shall be no more, neither shall there be mourning, nor crying, nor pain anymore, for the former things have passed away." Revelation 20:11-15, 21:1-5

If you don't have the assurance of your place in the new creation re-read this chapter. Thank you for reading to the end. Please write a review on Amazon.com.

Appendix About the author: Charlie Liebert's biography, publications, careers, Christian testimony, writing & publications.

For more info go to http://www.sixdaycreation.com or send your comments to charlie@sixdaycreation.com

Appendix About the Author.
Charlie's Biography.

Charlie Liebert grew up in Amityville, Long Island and lived in the New York/New Jersey area until 1973. When he, with his wife Terry, and their two children, relocated to Greensboro, NC. After his high school graduation in 1959, he received an AAS degree in Chemical Technology from the State University of New York at Farmingdale.

From 1961 to 1967, he worked for Lever Brothers Company in their Research and Development Division doing laundry detergent application research, development, and product testing. In 1967, Charlie earned a BS in Chemistry from Fairleigh Dickenson University in Teaneck, NJ.

In 1967 he joined Geigy Chemical Corporation (which became CIBA-Geigy in 1970) advancing from laboratory technician to lab manager. In 1972 he received an MBA in Marketing from the Graduate Division of Iona College (New Rochelle, NY). In 1973, he moved from the research laboratory to the marketing department, where management responsibilities included market research, customer service, order processing, transportation, technology development, strategic planning, systems design, and budgeting. He retired in November 1994 at age 53.

Charlie's published numerous articles and editorials in both local and national publications. In 1984 he wrote a booklet about the decline of American public education, titled: *The Subversion of the INNOCENTS: What Happened to Our Schools*. Charlie has made over 400 presentations to groups such as the NC Governor's School, civic clubs (Kiwanis, Civitan, Rotary and many others), PTAs and public and private schools. He's conducted half-day workshops for homeschool students called *"Creation, Dinosaurs, and the Flood."* For several years he was on call to lead workshops and seminars for *"Answers in Genesis"* (Ken Ham's ministry).

Terry, his wife, worked for Weight Watchers in North Carolina for 25 years until they moved to Carlisle Pennsylvania in 2016. Both their children graduated high school from Wesleyan Education Center in High Point, NC. Melanie is married and a graduate in primary education from Messiah College in Grantham, PA. She taught second grade in a Christian school in Carlisle, PA and now teaches Kindergarten at that same school. Charlie and Terry have five grandchildren, Melanie, and Mike, live in Carlisle, and have a daughter, Alyssa and two sons, Jeffery, and Colson.

When Charlie became a Christian in 1977, he faced a severe intellectual dilemma. He had been taught evolution as a fact, yet when he read Genesis he saw, God created the world in six days a relatively short time ago. For three years, after his conversion, Charlie studied books by many "recent creationists" and became convinced that recent creation made a lot more sense than old age evolution. He says, "When you look at the science objectively recent Creation is much more viable than Evolution. I 'evolved' from an Old Earth Atheistic Evolutionist to a Young Earth Creationist in about three years."

In 1996 Charlie joined the board of Caldwell Classical Christian Academy in Greensboro and helped guide the school during its early years. In the academic year of 97-98, Charlie left the board to teach science and Bible in the Dialectic (Middle) school at Caldwell. In June of 1998, he began leading "Creation, Dinosaurs and the Flood" workshops and seminars. In 1998 six half-hour television programs, filmed in 1997, featuring Charlie, were consolidated into two 90-minute videos, and marketed worldwide by American Portrait Films.

They are *Creation Science with Charlie Liebert* and *Creation Geology with Charlie Liebert.*

From January 1995 to December 2005, Charlie produced a television series from his workshops and seminars for Greensboro Community Television called "*Creation Foundation Explanation.*" As a result of the TV show, he became known in Greensboro as the "Creation Guy." From August 1996 to June 1999 Charlie taught science programs for grades K through 6 at Caldwell Academy. Beginning in August 2004 Charlie began teaching at Davidson County Community College (DCCC), including Business Law, Study Skills, Introduction to Business, Principles of Management, and other business-related courses.

In early 2013 Charlie began his career as an author. The next section itemizes all the books published by Charlie including both those he wrote and those published for other authors. Date September 2, 2022.

Charlie Liebert's Books

Creative Historic Non-Fiction — Liebert Family History 1898-1950

Dramatic Fiction — Yellowstone's Child, NY Terrorist Attack

Christian Education — Parent's Guide, Biblical Creation

Christian Apologetics — Evangelism, Q & A, Evolution Critiqued

Christian Apologetics

1. *Always Be Ready to Give an Answer! A Former Atheist's Personal Christian Evangelism Plan."* Christian, do the "hard" questions you're asked stop you from being effective for Christ? Here's a strategy that will transform you into a fearless evangelist!

2. *12 Lesson Study Guide for Always Be Ready to Give an Answer.* Group study, mentoring, Sunday School, etc.

3. Charlie's Short Course in Evangelism. By Charlie Liebert. Based on Always Be Ready to Give an Answer.

4. ANSWERS For "The Hope That Is in You. Direct, Simple Answers to the World's "Hard Questions" Christian, do you want answers to those "hard" questions your friends and family ask? Charlie answers more than 100 questions in short, clear answers and explains why Evolution fails. These Q&A were adapted from my website:

5. *Without 3 Miracles Darwin's Dead! Science Proves Atheistic Evolution is IMPOSSIBLE."* because it violates three scientific laws: the 1st Law (Something from Nothing), 2nd Law (Entropy) and the Law of Biogenesis (Life from Dead Stuff).

6. *Charlie's Christian Apologetic's Blogs.* Biblical Truth and Science in 3 Years of Blogs.

7. *Roman Centurions' Stories.* Jesus' life as seen by Judea's Occupiers.

Christian Education

8. *My Children's Christian Education, What Should I Do? A Christian Educators Analysis and Advice.* Shows the Biblical Mandate to educate your Christian children and gives you an organized method to implement it by explaining ALL the educational options available in the US today. You know your own family situation so you must choose which of these options are best to educate your children.

9. *God's Created Creatures Wreck Evolution.* Teaching Guide to Biblical Creation. 8X10 full color

10. *Agony of Three Griefs More! Christian Parents' Compound Grief for Our Son's Suicide.* By Charlie Liebert. With Cindie Brown, Liz Woolley, and Darren Shell

General Literature. Fiction

11. *Yellowstone's Child.* Kidnapped at 10 with complete amnesia she recovers her memory at 22 after she's become a millionaire and successful TV star. She asks: "Who am I? Sarah Johanson, Sally Graham, Sally Johnson, or Detective Elaine Scott." NO! She answers, "I'm Yellowstone's Child". Rated "G." Great story for teens. Large print and Screen Play versions available.

12. *The Memory Tree, A Gospel Christmas Story.* A great read for families at Christmas gatherings that takes 15-20 minutes to read. For all ages. It clearly presents the Gospel of Jesus Christ.

13. *One Android, 399 lives – 59th Street Terror Attack Kills 399.* Fictional terrorist attack with a passenger airplane in NY city. Although not specifically Christian it includes two Appendices that are instructive in evangelism.

14. *Tales of a Teen Aristocrat, Pranksters, a Witch, Curses, Ghosts, and a Jew.* Composite of Liebert family history with the family specific details removed that are not of interest to the public. This book contains all three stories listed below

    15. *Rosemarie, Kristallnacht Transformation.* My twice Jewish aunt, with a Jewish father and a Jewish husband, survived the Holocaust in Germany 1937-1945 by becoming, Olga, her dead Gentile cousin.

    16. *Helene [Hel-lain-a] at Mama Henney's Boarding School for Girls.* My grandmother's adventures as a 16 to18-year-old at an all-girls school for aristocrats in 1900 northern Italy.

    17. *The Curse of the Witch of Zahlendorf. Der Fluch der Hexe von Zahlendorf.* A 17th-century German folk tale dramatically illustrated by events in 1921.

Charlie's Publishing Assistance

1. *Your Son Did Not Die in Vain. A true story about the devastating effects of video gaming addiction.* By Liz Wooley with John Langel, Sr. Two versions: 8X10 full color and 6X9 B&W

2. *Business Principles That Honor God, Worldwide! Startups, Operations, Successes and Failures.* By Edward S Rowse 6X9 B&W

3. *POPS an Autobiography of a Grandfather.* Legacy Biography by Dan Kovlak. 6X9 B&W

4. *Selling From Your Soul.* By John M. Langel, St., Coauthor Lyndon B Risser 6X9 B&W Unpublished as of July 2022

5. *The Rescued Cat That Was Chipped.* By Debi McBride, Illustrations by Sarita Ricchiuto. 8X10 full color

6. *The Toxic Dangers of Video Games. Things you need to know about video games and the internet.* By Liz Wooley and John Langel, Sr. 8X10 full color.

7. *Leave 'Em in the Dust. Following Jesus in Missions.* By Jim Douglas 6X9 B&W

8. *As Luck Would Have It... And Then Again...* by Stan Silverman 6X9 eBook, Paperback and Hard Covers

9. *Louie Lighthouse Book Series* by Terry Webb. Five in set.

    10. Manning the Light eBook and 6X9 Paperback

    11. Weathering the Storms eBook and 6X9 Paperback

    12. Mystery and Mishap. eBook and 6X9 Paperback

    13. Leaving the Light. eBook and 6X9 Paperback

    14. LLB Series Study Guide, eBook and 8 ½ X 11 paperback

15. *Anxiety in the Classroom: Evaluating the Relationship Between Instructor Immediacy and Public Speaking Anxiety Among College Students.* By Russ Kulp. 6X9 Paperback and eBook

16. *Remembering Stephen.* By Cindie Brown with Scot Brown and Charlie Liebert.

17. *in the chips. The Life and Times of Adolph Dioda.* By Olivia Dioda Fox

18.

Charlie's Many Different Careers. (Text)

I began my working life at the age of 16. In 1957, I went to work as a stock and clean up boy for McCrory-McLellan (a retailer called in those days a "Five and Dime Store"). I worked part time for the time it took to finish high school in 1959 and complete my AAS degree at State University of New York (SUNY) at Farmingdale in June 1961.

In September 1961, I took a job at Lever Brothers R&D center in Edgewater New Jersey. I left my parents' home and went out on my own. I worked at Lever as a laboratory technician and then a product-testing supervisor for the six years it took to get my BS in Chemistry at Fairleigh Dickenson University in Teaneck NJ. I worked 40 hours per week and went to college at night.

After graduating, I changed jobs and companies to J.R. Geigy Chemical Company in Ardsley NY working as a research chemist. I married Terry Lee Perrone from West New York, New Jersey and we moved to Rockland County, NY. I soon realized if I wanted to get far with a career in chemistry, I would have to get both a master's and a Ph.D. I believed that was too much educational work, so I decided to change my educational direction from science to business and studied for an MBA in Marketing at Iona College's Graduate Division of Business in New Rochelle, NY.

When I got my Masters, in June 1970, I was immediately assigned the job of coordinating the CIBA-Geigy Chemicals Division move from Ardsley, NY to Greensboro, North Carolina. The division and my family moved to Greensboro in late 1973.

After the relocation finished, I was assigned a job as Business Planner for the Dye and Chemicals Division of CIBA-Geigy Corp. In 1975 the company embarked on a major program to acquire companies to expand our division's business. I was selected to lead this team as Acquisition Coordinator. During this acquisition program, we purchased two businesses and one product line. In March 1977

I became a Christian and later in the year later Terry also became a Christian. I was 35 years old. The story of my conversion to Christ from a hardcore Atheist is in my testimony that follows.

When the acquisition program finished in 1978, I moved to Greenville, SC as Information Systems Director in one of the companies we had acquired. We returned to Greensboro, NC in 1980 and I became Manager of Customer Service. I managed Customer Service until 1988, when I became Manager of Business Planning. I took a retirement package from CIBA-Geigy in 1994. During my years with CG, at the various times, I managed between 2 and 35 people. When working in acquisitions and customer service, I often flew 4 to 8 times a week.

In 1990, while still working full time, I joined the board of Caldwell Academy-A Classical Christian School founded in 1988. After I had retired in 1996, I resigned from the Caldwell Board so I could teach Dialectic Science (Middle School) for one year. From 1996 until 1999 I led weekly science assembly programs at Caldwell.

In 1997, I went to work for Answers in Genesis- Ken Ham's ministry. For two years, leading programs with both children's workshops and adult seminars.

Starting in 1995, for almost a decade, I produced a one-hour weekly public access TV show on Greensboro Community Television (GCTV) using footage shot from my seminars and workshops. Immediately after I retired in 1994, I began a single proprietorship business called Creation, Dinosaurs, and thE Flood (CDEF). CDEF hosted workshops and seminars selling books and videos at these programs and 3-4 homeschool conventions each year. Credit card processing and a web site was a part of CDEF's operations http://www.sixdaycreation.com that posted my GCTV videos and answered questions from web surfers.

In 2001, I gave up selling books and sold only video products until 2011 when the business was liquidated.

In August 2004, I began teaching business courses at Davidson County Community College including Principles of Management, Introduction to Business, Business Law, Principles of Marketing, Study Skills, Student Success Strategies, and other business subjects. While at DCCC, I worked with both Blackboard and Moodle learning platforms. During my time at DCCC, I won 2 academic prizes for excellence in teaching, including a grant for $3,000. I began work as fiction and non-fiction author in 2012.

In 2012 I started my career as an author and publisher which is covered in an earlier section of this appendix. By 2022 I published more than 30 books using Amazon's, Kindle Direct Publishing. I wrote about half of them, and the rest are other authors' work.

Charlie's Many Different Careers. (Table)

Company	Career	Start	End
McCrory-McLellan	Stock and Clean-up Boy	1957	1961
State University NY	AAS Chemical Technology	1959	1961
Lever Bros R&D	Laboratory Technician	1961	1964
Lever Bros R&D	Product Testing Supervisor	1964	1967
Fairleigh Dickenson	BS in Chemistry	1961	1966
J.R. Geigy Co.	Research Chemist	1967	1970
Iona, Graduate Division	MBA Marketing & Econometrics	1967	1970
CIBA-Geigy Co	Greensboro Relocation Coordinator	1970	1973
CIBA-Geigy Co	Business Planner D&C Division	1973	1975
CIBA-Geigy Co	D&C Acquisition Team Leader	1975	1978
Jesus' Church	Became a Christian 3/20/1977	1977	Eternity
Charles Tanner	Information Systems Director	1978	1980
CIBA-Geigy Co	Customer Service Manager	1980	1988
CIBA-Geigy Co	Business Planning Manager	1988	1994
CIBA-Geigy Co	Retired, November 1994	1994	Present

Creation, Dinosaurs the Flood (CDEF)	Workshops, Youth "Talk Back" and Seminars. Sole Proprietor Business	1994	2011
Greensboro NC Community TV	Directed and produced Weekly TV show	1995	2005
Caldwell CC Academy	Board Member	1996	1998
Answers in Genesis	Seminar/Workshop Leader	1997	1999
Caldwell CC Academy	Science Teacher, Gr 1-8	1998	2001
Davidson Cnty. Com College	Adjunct Instructor Business Law, etc.	2004	2018
Author	Fiction/Non-Fiction Author	2012	Present
Published 1st Book	Always Be Ready to Give an Answer!	2012	2013
Published 2nd Book	ANSWERS For: "The Hope That Is in You"	2012	2014
Published 5 Kindle eBooks and Stories	Helene, Yellowstone's Child, One Android 399 Lives, Rosemarie & Memory Tree	2013	2015
Published 3rd Book	Without 3 Miracles Darwin's DEAD!	2013	2017
Convert to KDP	All books	2016	2018
Publish Books Charlie Liebert	Paperbacks, eBooks, and Hardbacks	2018	Present
Publishing Assistance	Paperbacks, eBooks, and Hardbacks	2018	Present

Charlie's Christian Testimony.

I grew up in a small town, Amityville on Long Island, NY, with my two sisters, Rosemarie, and Joyce. My parents took us to church almost every Sunday. In Sunday school, we learned many Bible stories, but I never remembered being confronted with the Gospel. At 16 years old, I became aware of the hypocrisy of church members. In church one Sunday morning, the pastor was droning on about the evil of drinking. I knew that most of the adults sitting around me had been at the Amityville Yacht Club season-opening the night before and had consumed a lot of beer, wine, and liquor. How foolish I thought. "These people don't believe a word of what's being said! Hypocrites!" I shut off anything the church had to say and began my descent from Marginal Christianity into Atheism.

By the time I was 24 and approaching completion of my BS in Chemistry, I had become an active hardcore Atheist. I was living in New Jersey and met my future wife, Terry, through one of my roommates who was her cousin. Weekends were spent visiting both our families. My wife is of Italian descent and has a large family. Sundays were often spent in great feasts at her Aunt Tessie's, with 20 or 30 people. We married, in a Roman Catholic Church, to please her family, had our first child and moved to Rockland County NY.

Although marriage had brought some changes, I was falling more and more into sinful practices. We had our second child and the company I worked for moved us to Greensboro, NC. By this time, I had become addicted to pornography and was well on the way to alcohol dependency. Terry and I had a long argument in January 1977 and unknown to me, she called out, "God help me and help my marriage." We talked about divorce. My life was coming apart, and there seemed to be nothing I could do about it. We lost all the Sunday family gatherings when we moved, and Sunday became a barren time.

Most of our new neighbors and fellow workers, in Greensboro, went to church so Terry decided to attend an Episcopal church, leaving me at home with two young children. I didn't like managing the children alone, so I decided to visit this church with her. I had no interest in anything the church had to say, but the people were friendly. Social activities were fun, but Sunday morning was dull.

The Episcopal Church was a good place for Terry, the ex-Catholic and Charlie, the ex-Methodist; now Atheist to go. Nothing came from the pulpit that challenged either one of us. There were, however, three families in that church whose lives were different, very different. I couldn't explain then, why, or how, but they were.

We attended a Bible study with them called Edge of Adventure and our marriage relationship improved for a short time. The study was over, and we went back to the way it was, bad! I was promoted at work and went to work for a man I despised. My life seemed to be coming apart both at home and at work and there was nothing I could seem to do about it. One of the men from that study group suggested I attend a men's weekend retreat in Asheville, NC in early 1977. Terry encouraged me to go. After all, it was a chance to get away from all my problems. So, I went!

At the beginning of the weekend, on Thursday night, we gave up our watches so we would not be able to keep track of time. We took a vow of silence until breakfast Friday, which gave us some time to think. Friday morning, after breakfast the first speaker asked three questions; "What is your purpose in life? Where are you going? What does it all mean?" As I sat there, I realized I had no answers. Yes, I had a wife, two children, a house, two cars, but I knew that was not the

175

answer. These questions bothered me. After many talks, I hardly remembered. I went into the chapel alone on Saturday night because of the issues raised by that first talk and the impending disaster of my life, I knelt and began to think and remember.

I remembered my high school friend, Frank telling me when I was working on my MBA about how Jesus had changed his life when he'd lost everything. Then I remembered sitting in the apartment in New Jersey, before I met Terry, with my other roommates, drinking beer and watching Billy Graham on TV. We made great fun of his telling. We were lost sinners and needed Jesus, but now Jesus somehow seemed real. I said in my mind, "God, if you're real, (I wasn't sure if he was), you can have my life because it is an awful mess. God faithful to his Word took it. In the next moments, there was someone in the room with me that I could not see, but I felt His presence. Something strange had happened, and I had no clue yet what it was.

When I came back home to Greensboro, I came down into the den where Terry was watching TV. Her first reaction was: "What happened to you. Did you see God?" I wasn't sure. I immediately developed an adamant desire to read the Bible. As I got back into my daily routine, I asked the friend that had invited me to the retreat weekend where I should start reading the Bible. He suggested the Gospel of John.

When I got to John, Chapter 3 where Nicodemus encounters Jesus I read about being born again. I called my friend at 2:00 AM and asked, "Was I born again?" He confirmed that was what had happened. God now began to change all aspects of my life. Our marriage began to heal. I was growing in Christ daily and my knowledge of the scriptures was rapidly increasing.

Terry would become a Christian three months later, and we would then begin to grow together. She went to the same retreat weekend for women that I had attended. She was confronted with the Gospel on Thursday evening when they walked through the "stations of the cross." Her Catholic upbringing came back in a rush. She always knew she was not worthy but had never understood the solution. Giving her testimony she says, "It's as if God was saying to me, Terry, give me your sins because that's why I died." I went to pick her up so I could attend the closing ceremony. She did not expect me. When I came into the room, our eyes met, and I instantly knew that she knew what I knew. God had redeemed another sinner.

We went into the chapel for the closing. I had fasted all the time she was at the weekend (I didn't have diabetes yet). No one told me you had to drink a lot of water when fasting, so as I found out later, I was severely dehydrated. We went into the chapel, knelt like a good Episcopalian and the closing began. The central part of this ceremony is the leader asking the new initiates to ask God the question, "God what do you want from me?" As Terry asked that question, I passed out in a dead faint. She thought God took ME! Of course, I revived, and we returned home. God had made us both new in Christ. The Bible says, "Therefore if anyone is in Christ, he is a new creation. The old has passed away; behold, the new has come." (I Corinthians 5:17)

During the following weeks we continued to attend the Episcopal Church, but realized we weren't getting any spiritual nourishment. We met with the priest and here is the dialogue as I remember it:

Terry: "We'd like to see more Bible taught here."

Priest: "The Bible is too controversial to teach any more than we do."

Charlie: "Something radical happened to us. Can you explain it?" (We were both born again, and by now we knew it.)

Priest: "You had an emotional experience. You'll get over it!" (It's more than 40 years later, and I still haven't gotten over it and don't expect to!)

We realized very quickly we had to find another church. We found it through those three couples from our first Bible study. For the first time, since our conversions, we heard preaching from Scripture. "Halleluiah, what a Savior!" was the first hymn we sang in that new church. Boy! That struck a chord.

God next took us to Greenville, SC in 1978 when CIBA-Geigy bought a small subsidiary. I was asked to bring its computer systems up to our company's standards. After we moved, we started to look for a church to attend. We visited several different mainline denomination churches that were dead. Both of us recognized the need for spiritual food and it wasn't there. We also visited a wild charismatic church and that didn't work either. We became increasingly frustrated by not finding any place that preached the Word and had spiritual life. I went to work one Monday feeling very down about our church hunting. One of the people I worked with was a Jewish engineer from Brooklyn, NY. At lunch, we were talking, and my church problem came up. He said with a twinkle in his eye, "Charlie, I know just the church for you." I said, "How can you, a Jew, know what church would be right for me, a Christian?" He said, "Because they are about as obnoxious about Christ as you are." So, a Jew, one of God's chosen by the flesh, led us to Mitchell Road Presbyterian Church (MRPC) which we joined immediately.

While in Greenville, before work on Tuesdays, I attended a Bible study with other men from MRPC. One Tuesday was a holiday, and so because we didn't have to go to work, we all sat around having a second cup of coffee enjoying the great fellowship. A new believer in the group asked the teacher, "Dean, tell us some great spiritual nuggets." Dean thought for several minutes and then said: "I'll give you two." First, he began to sing the children's song "Jesus loves me" and quickly we all joined in. Next, he hesitated and with a serious look on his face said: "There is a chorus from a hymn that sums it all up. 'Trust and obey for there's no other way to be happy in Jesus than to trust and obey.'" Those two thoughts have stuck with me my whole Christian life. "Because Jesus loves me, I will trust and obey! There is no other way!"

Soon after we arrived in Greenville, Terry tried to register our children in the local public school. On three separate occasions, she was unable to register them. The pastor from MRPC came to visit us the week before school was to begin to encourage us to enroll our children in MRPC's Christian School. I remember Dr. Thomas Cross saying, "As Christians, you want to bring your covenant children up in the faith and become believers as you are." Christian School will be consistent with everything you teach them at home. Since public schools' foundation is Humanism, when you put them there, you bring them into the camp of the enemy for 5 hours a day. Most parents can't or won't undo the daily damage done in those schools. We began our commitment to educating our children in a Christian school.

After we had been in MRPC for more than a year Terry and I were asked to help start a mission church in nearby Simpsonville. I had been trained and ordained as a Deacon and then as an Elder. Three Elders, John Wheeler, Render Cains, and I were the founding elders of Davenport Road Presbyterian Church. One of my responsibilities was teaching the high school class. One Sunday the lesson was on Jesus' teaching about building your house on the rock or the sand from Matthew

Matthew 7:24-27 "Everyone then who hears these words of mine and does them will be like a wise man who built his house

179

on the rock. And the rain fell, and the floods came, and the winds blew and beat on that house, but it did not fall, because it had been founded on the rock. And everyone who hears these words of mine and does not do them will be like a foolish man who built his house on the sand. And the rain fell, and the floods came, and the winds blew and beat against that house, and it fell, and great was the fall of it."

The lesson included little paper houses and pages with pictures of sand and rock. I thought this is a weak childish lesson, BUT I taught it faithfully. I even told Terry on the ride home that I thought it was a stupid lesson. Years later when we were back in Greensboro, I met one of the students from that class. He said, "Mr. Liebert, do you remember teaching the lesson about the two houses, one built on sand and the other built on rock?" I confirmed I remembered. "Well, that lesson changed my life!" Lesson learned by me! NEVER underestimate God's ability to use weak vessels to carry out his will and don't trust your sinful judgment to sell God's word short!

While at MRPC we met many missionaries and had several opportunities to support them. More than a year after we started to attend MRPC a college student came to visit us who was taking a short-term mission's trip to South America. She told us she needed just $50 more to meet her expenses for the trip. I said, of course, we'd give her the $50 and wrote her a check right then. When she left, Terry became very upset about my giving her $50. Terry was right I had no idea where we'd get the money. We had some extraordinary expenses in the last two months including paying the deductible on a minor auto accident Terry had several months before. When I left for work that Monday, she was still quite upset about my "giving away $50." As I drove to work, I considered if I should not have done it, but I couldn't come to a clear answer. "Yes, I wanted to help the student go, No I did not have the money" At about 11:00 that morning after I had just come out of a meeting my phone rang. It was Terry. I could tell by her voice something was up. She said: "I have to apologize for getting upset about the $50." I said: "Why?" "About 10:00 a man came to the door from the insurance company and gave me a check for $75 for the accident. God gave us the $50." I added: "And a $25 bonus." James says: "Faith without works is dead." So, the Word came back: "Because Jesus loves me, I will trust and obey! There is no other way!"

We came back to Greensboro in 1980 and were there until we moved to Carlisle Pennsylvania in September 2016. While in Greensboro we were members of Providence OPC and now In Carlisle, we are members of Redeemer OPC.

68342803R00102